# FLY-FISHING
# Heresies

# FLY-FISHING
# Heresies

A new gospel
for American anglers

## Leonard M. Wright, Jr.
## foreword by Nick Lyons

Stoeger Publishing Company

Some of the material in this book has been printed previously in *American Sportsman*, *Esquire*, *Field & Stream*, *Fishing World*, *Random Casts*, *Signature*, *Sports Afield*, and *The Anglers' Club of New York Bulletin*.

The author wishes to thank the following for their contributions of photographs: William Aller, Wesley Balz, Bob Elman, Andrew Kner, and Shirley Wright.

ISBN: 0-88317-083-3

Published by Stoeger Publishing Company
55 Ruta Court
South Hackensack, New Jersey 07606

First Stoeger quality paperback edition, January 1978

This Stoeger Sportsman's Library Edition is published
by arrangement with Winchester Press

Distributed to the book trade by Follett Publishing
Company, 1010 West Washington Boulevard, Chicago,
Illinois 60607 and to the sporting goods trade by
Stoeger Industries, 55 Ruta Court, South Hackensack,
New Jersey 07606

In Canada, distributed to the book trade and to the
sporting goods trade by Stoeger Trading Company,
900 Ontario Street East, Montreal, Quebec H2L 1P4

Printed in the United States of America

# Contents

# FOREWORD

## Leonard Wright:
## The Angler as Iconoclast
### by Nick Lyons

In the midst of debunking one or the other of fly-fishing's hallowed traditions, Leonard Wright asks simply: "But shouldn't fly-fishing be a joy as well as a challenge?" Not one or the other but both—for a challenge unleavened by pleasure becomes a stale mania, and a joy without a challenge wears as thin as hedonism. Part of both, for Wright, is being radically independent—taking one's joys and challenges on one's own terms, free from what one has read, free from the shackles of what someone else has legislated as the only "right" way.

If one of the abiding pleasures of fly-fishing has been its discrete traditions, an equally delicious sport, when supported by common sense, is breaking them. Wright does so with relish. The saints—Halford and Walton—short rods, dead drift, and a host of other sacred cows and mores and techniques draw his fearless blows. But Wright is not merely pugnacious: He is brilliant, full of common sense and uncommon ingenuity, and he is one of the happiest and most thorough-going iconoclasts in the tradition of angling.

Consider his attack on one of the newer orthodoxies: that it is sportier to fish with a short, light rod than with a long, heavier one. Heading briskly wrongwards down what might seem a one-way street, and blithely referring to a "36-ounce beauty" of a rod with a "light, flexible tip," Wright calls the short rod "the least effective, least comfortable, least 'sporting' fly-fishing tool ever invented for fishing running water. I know it's risky to knock another man's woman, dog, or favorite rod, but look at the evidence." And then he proceeds to show precisely *how* the short rod is ineffective and uncomfortable, and your doubts turn to intense interest as he eloquently extols the virtues of the longer rods he uses.

Nothing is sacrosanct before Wright's penetrating eye. He even scores the revered Walton—whose influence, he says, "is almost as strong and all-pervading as original sin"—for his *style* as well as his angling ability and ethics. And labels him a plagiarist, to boot. He pushes not only the "sudden inch" for caddis but also jiggled mayflies—and the logic of casting dry flies across and *down*stream. He sees many modern nymphal imitations as being "as realistic as the figures in Mme. Tussaud's waxworks" but "as stiff as boards," and asks us to reconsider the recently discarded wet-fly patterns as more effective. Invariably, his suggestions are the product of careful observation; the Quill Gordon, he notes, "leaves its nymphal shuck on the river floor and ascends through the water to the surface as a winged adult"—making any nymph a poor choice.

Admirers of Wright's first book, *Fishing the Dry Fly as a Living Insect,* will welcome his additional information on the now-much-less-neglected fluttering caddis. There are more tying instructions, more valuable suggestions on technique. But he is more than an Apostle for Trichoptera. There is some marvelous information here on increasing trout populations by improving rivers; some memorable glimpses of the once-extraordinary fly-fishing on Austria's Traun River as well as the intriguing pleasures of "backyard fishing"; a convincing invitation to fish "slower and lower" for big salmon and to use imitations of crane flies, house-flies, wasps, bees, and flying ants for summer trout; and a glorious paean to "the perfect fish," the Salmo family.

Leonard Wright admits that he's been a "compulsive fisherman" ever since he could walk. He's also become a uniquely observant, and articulate fisherman. He's come to recognize that, "Obviously, trout aren't as gullible as people. You can't fool all of the fish some of the time or even some of the fish all of the time."

*Fly-Fishing Heresies*, for all its hard looks at past and reigning orthodoxies, remains devoted to sharing the fruit of very real trial-and-error experimentation. It *will* help you catch more of the trout more of the time.

Happily, the ways of trout and salmon will always remain something of a mystery; we'll never be able to gull them all the time. That's the source of both the joy and the challenge of fly-fishing. But fishing through this book with Len Wright will make flyfishermen less gullible and more observant—and hopefully encourage more of that independent, iconoclastic spirit which is his.

*Nick Lyons*
*New York City*
*September 1, 1975*

"Heresies" is a strong word. It smacks of blasphemy, sacrilege, and worse. How could it possibly be applied to what Walton called "the blameless sport"? Especially in these days of "do-your-own-thing" values?

Easily.

Perhaps the only solid establishment left today is made up of the fly-fishing followers of the nearly sainted Frederick M. Halford. They still believe unswervingly in three major tenets proclaimed by the Master from England nearly ninety years ago.

The first of these was that dry-fly fishing is an enjoyable and productive way to take brown trout. To this, I can only say "Amen."

But the corollary pontifications seem suspect to me. The two most influential were that the artificial fly must be fished without any motion (or absolutely "dead drift") and that the artificial is increasingly more effective as it nears the exact photographic imitation of the natural fly.

Several years ago I wrote a book questioning the dead-drift dogma. In *Fishing the Dry Fly as a Living Insect* I attempted to prove that a little carefully controlled manipulation increased the appeal of a dry fly much, perhaps most, of the time.

Reactions were mixed. A few wrote that they already knew

this. Many said that this technique and the recommended "fluttering caddis" imitations had increased their catches considerably. But the establishment was not moved.

Shortly after publication I bumped into Sparse Grey Hackle— dean of American fly-fishing authors and Boswell of the purist fraternity. "Congratulations, Len," he said. "I see you've written an entire book devoted to the ancient art of trolling." I could see the twinkle behind his glasses, but I could also feel the needle in the words of this, one of the kindest of men.

In the *Fly-Fishing Heresies* launched on the following pages I add arguments against the "dead-drift" doctrine, challenge "exact imitation," and attempt to topple some neo-Halfordian beliefs—ones that have since been added by the faithful. After you've read them, perhaps you will reflect and experiment. If these chapters open your mind to new suppositions and start you theorizing on why a trout does, indeed, take a counterfeit fly, then angling will be the richer for it.

Consider this book, then, as opening remarks to a jury. Not as a verdict. That last word will always come from the final judge, the fish.

*Leonard M. Wright, Jr.*
*New York City*
*September 1, 1975*

# FLY-FISHING
# Heresies

# 1

# A Dry-Fly Heresy

Fishing for trout with the floating fly, as it is practiced and preached in America today, has become as highly ritualized a performance as bullfighting. Both pursuits are straitjacketed by rigid rules, hobbled by out-of-date choreography, and bear little relevance to the final downfall of the quarry.

I'm not an expert on the efficient slaughter of beef cattle, but I think I may be of some help to dry-fly fishermen, all of whom, as far as I know, would like to catch more trout whether they creel them or release them. For the fact is, I have stumbled onto a far more effective way to take trout on the floating fly. Very likely, others have, too, but since no one has written it up yet as far as I know, I'll make the first cast.

To witness the classic style of American dry-fly fishing that I have become disenchanted with, just drive along any first-rate trout stream once the spring invasion of hatchery trucks and bait-fishers is over. You will soon see at least one man dressed in what looks like the bottom half of a diving suit, waving a long, limber rod. His thick, oily fly line hisses gently as it doubles back on itself, straightens, then loops forward again, darting his small fly out toward a chosen patch of water. You will notice he is casting in an upstream direction so that his fly will float back toward him freely on the current; but this is not nearly as simple as it looks.

The angler has to calculate the effect of current tongues and eddies and cunningly curve or "S" his line onto the water so that the hidden hands in the flow won't pluck his fly off-course from a true, dead-drift float. This unnatural pull would be drag — the dry-fly man's archenemy. He avoids this as the golfer fights looking up or as the skier tries to keep his weight off the inside ski. And it is this ability to achieve a drag-free presentation that separates the true flyfisher from the mere flogger.

After a few seconds of pure float, the angler will snap his line off the water, dry his fly by false-casting it in the air, then send it out to search a new section of the surface. He will repeat this process again and again as he works slowly upstream until he disappears from view or until his rhythm is interrupted by the strike of a trout.

There's an almost ballet-like beauty to this performance and it tends to hypnotize the fisherman, but it doesn't seem to have as telling an effect on the trout. I know because I spent many years acquiring this classical skill, and many more practicing it, and it just doesn't work very well or very often. The reason for this is that most of our natural aquatic insects do *not* float serenely downstream like priceless objects of art. They twitch, flutter, struggle, and skitter before they manage to take off, and our trout seem to know this only too well.

If you watch a trout pool carefully when only a few insects are hatching, you'll see what I mean. Especially on cool or rainy days when takeoffs are difficult, a fly will float down-current a hundred feet or more over the best lies, unmolested, only to be eaten when it makes its first fluttering attempts to get airborne. Yet, only a few moments later, a fly of the same species that starts struggling as soon as it emerges will be taken instantly by a fish that let the previous free-floater pass by. I have seen this happen so regularly that I am convinced this is the rule rather than the exception. The example I just referred to involved mayflies. Caddis flies, the other important order of aquatic insects, are notoriously active when on the water, and it was by trying to imitate them that I finally strayed from the paths of orthodoxy.

Another thing you'll notice while watching such a pool is that virtually all hatching or egg-laying insects will head up-current unless there is a disastrous downstream wind. This tropism is crucial to the perpetuation of the species: So many lumbering nymphs and larvae are washed downstream by floods that the headwaters would soon be depopulated if each generation of winged adults didn't leapfrog back upriver.

Trout are carnivores, and it is motion that most often helps them separate the meat from the chaff that the current brings their way. A bewildering variety of objects, both animal and vegetable, passes over a trout's head all day long during summer. The length of this inventory impresses me every time I hold a piece of cheesecloth in the tongue of a current for a few minutes. Along with the bees, wasps, houseflies, beetles, leaf hoppers, ants, and aquatic insects strained out, I find an equal quantity of small twigs, leaf cuttings, petals, berries, hemlock needles, and assorted debris nearly the same size, color, and shape as the edible insects themselves. Trout can tell the difference, though, without studying entomology and botany. Insects wiggle, hemlock needles don't.

Trout, especially wild trout, make this distinction between food and trash almost unerringly. I have tossed a wide assortment of likely looking objects to feeding trout from a concealed position and had not more than one halfhearted take out of a hundred samples while that same fish rose, from time to time, to a great variety of windfall insects. Those twigs, leaf bits, and small pebbles you find in trout stomachs? Don't let them mislead you. They're almost certainly pieces from the cases of caddis larvae—a favorite trout food that is grubbed off the bottom, abrasive house and all.

It stands to reason, then, that the angler will be more successful if his imitation duplicates not only the appearance of a natural insect, but its behavior pattern as well. A good example might be the case of a fisherman trying to cope with a caddis-fly hatch. This type of aquatic insect is nearly as important to trout as is the hallowed mayfly, though it is skimpily mentioned in most books on fly-fishing and is not closely imitated by any of our most popular flies. In fact, caddis flies are becoming even more impor-

A typical mayfly imitation with upright wings, slim, tapered body, and a tail representing the setae of the Ephemerae.

tant to the flyfisher because they're hardier than mayflies and can stand more of the pollution and deteriorating stream conditions that have plagued us for over a century.

Adult caddis look nothing at all like ninety-nine percent of our dry flies because the latter are patterned after mayflies. Caddis have no tails and fold their opaque wings in an inverted "V," horizontally, covering their bodies. Mayflies, like most of our artificials, have long tails and carry their translucent wings erect, like Marconi-rigged sails, above the body. The differences in the silhouettes of these two orders of insects are enormous. Caddis flies are extremely active both as they hatch out on the surface and when they return to the river later on for mating and egg laying. They twitch, flutter, and zigzag on the water surface in a distinctive manner that the trout find irresistible.

One of the most plentiful of our several hundred species of caddis is a medium-sized, brownish insect known as the shad fly. On some famous rivers like New York State's Beaverkill the shad fly is the most profuse single insect to appear each year, yet most anglers find it a frustrating fly. When this hatch is really on, fish will be rising in the runs and pools all up and down the river, yet most dry-fly men will be drawing blank, or nearly so. For some reason, there just isn't any available imitation that looks anything like this fly, but that's only part of the problem. More important, this insect does *not* float down-current with the statue-like poise of the classic dry fly. In fact, like most caddis, this insect seems to enjoy finding itself on the water as much as the average house cat does, and it protests nearly as vigorously.

Two nearly forgotten fishing techniques duplicated this behavior quite accurately, but, unfortunately, neither is effective with modern tackle. The practice of dapping — bouncing the fly over the surface on a very short line directly below the rod tip — was a telling technique three hundred years ago when fly rods were sixteen to eighteen feet long. With today's seven- to eight-

*Left:* a fiber-winged "fluttering caddis" with slim, downwinged silhouette. *Right:* a flat-winged stonefly artificial.

footers, dapping doesn't give the angler enough range to be useful except on small, brushed-over brooks. The same is true of dancing a dropper fly which has been tied a few feet up the leader. This second, airborne fly can be zigzagged and trickled over the surface when the rod is held high, but with today's equipment, fifteen to twenty feet is maximum range, and no self-respecting brown trout will allow the angler that close in clear, smooth water. Certainly our shorter rods dictate a whole new approach if the fly is to be manipulated effectively on the surface.

A method of manipulation that I worked out several years ago is surprisingly simple and effective. Since any motion imparted to the dry fly must be in an upstream direction or slower than the current, the way natural flies tend to move, I position myself above and across stream from the fish or its suspected lie. I then cast my caddis imitation three or four feet above the chosen spot, throwing a pronounced curve, bellying my line upstream. Within a second after the fly hits the water—before the leader or line tip can start to sink—I give my rod a short, sharp, upward twitch which sends the fly darting up current an inch or so. Then I feed out slack line and let the fly float, drag-free, for six or eight feet—enough and more to cover the lie of the fish. This "sudden inch" recreates the behavior of a winged caddis closely enough so that it will usually be taken if the presentation is made accurately and if the fly itself is a passing imitation of the caddis that are on the water.

This second "if" posed a problem even more difficult than that presentation one, though. Since the caddis, unlike the mayfly, has no tail, there is nothing to support the heaviest part of the hook which is directly over the bend. The only available caddis patterns with any semblance of realism — and even these are hard to come by in this country—are the English "sedges" which are winged with stiff feather sections laid tent-shaped along the body and finished off with conventional hackle at the head. This type of fly has an excellent silhouette and floats passably—if you fish it dead drift. Twitch it, though, and it sinks tail first.

Hours of tedious trial and error at the fly-tying bench finally produced a fly that seems to solve this problem. I have substituted, for the vulnerable plumage wings, clusters of steely cock's hackle fibers bunched on top and on the sides of the hook shank,

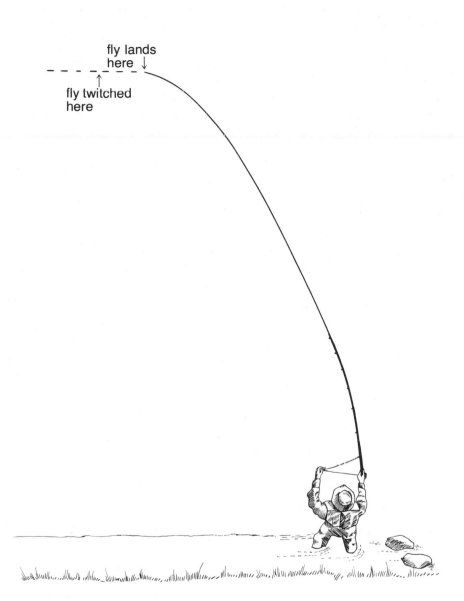

fly lands
here ↓

fly twitched
here

Aerial view of preferred presentation. Cast angled slightly downstream with a curve in the line. Fish sees fly first.

but still lying parallel to the body. The silhouette is very similar to the "sedge" from all angles to my eye and the trout seem to agree. The big blessing of this new fly is that it floats like a ping-pong ball. It should: The entire wing, which is nearly twice as long as the body, is composed of the most water-repellent feathers known and acts as the floatingest tail a fly ever had. I can twitch the devil out of this fly, and, unless the leader sinks and thus tends to pull the fly under, it will skitter buoyantly over the surface even on drizzly days.

Obviously, a fly shaped like this isn't a good match when mayflies are on the water, and when this occurs I go back to the conventionally tied imitations. There have been many attempts to better the basic style of mayfly introduced by Halford more than eighty-five years ago, but I have found them all, including my own innovations, inferior to the original. I do, however, use long-hackled, variant flies quite often—not because they are better imitations, but because they float higher and can stand more manipulation without sinking.

I consider this floatability important because I usually give some motion to my artificial mayflies as well as to the caddis flies. Observation has led me to believe that all but the luckiest mayflies kick and struggle sporadically before they get off the water. I therefore use much the same technique for imitating mayfly behavior as I use when caddis flies are on the water. I make the same across-and-downstream presentation followed by the twitch that I use when caddis are hatching and results are equally rewarding. However, when I'm using the easy-to-drown, conventional dry fly, I ease up on the manipulation. Merely rocking the fly on its hackle tips so that it twinkles in the surface film seems to be realistic enough, and I've found that this mini-manipulation is fully acceptable to the trout during mayfly hatches.

But important as caddis and mayflies are to our fishing and fascinating as it may be to try to match the hatch, the most important and prevalent fishing condition we all have to face today is the non-hatch. For days on end, during the summer months, there will be no hatch worth imitating even in the evening and even on some of our most famous trout streams. We are becoming a nation of prospectors, spending most of our hours trying to pound up non-rising fish. And it is precisely here that the fluttering fly really proves its worth: it can make a feast out of what is usually a near-famine. The moving fly not only spurs indifferent fish to the surface, but it also opens up more hours of the day and more parts of the stream to productive fishing.

Today, the choicest spots on most of our public waters are usually tenanted all day long. You're almost sure to find an angler stationed at the head of a pool where the incoming current slows and fans out and there's likely to be one or two in the pockets and runs above. But the slow part of the pool will probably be unoccupied except for the last few minutes in the evening. This type of water makes up more than half the total yardage on most of our rivers, and it is here that I've found I can enjoy my sport to the utmost without playing an abrasive game of musical chairs with my fellow fishermen.

Let's say that I've rigged up beside the river at three o'clock on a July afternoon. I will now carefully skirt the patient angler lodged at the head of the pool and step into the water a courteous distance below him. This leaves me alone on the body of the pool, a stretch of water one hundred and fifty yards long and a hundred feet wide which, incidentally, probably has not been thrashed for several hours.

Since this pool curves gently to the left, from a downstream-facing point of view, I position myself on the left bank or on the weak side of the current and prepare to prospect the deeper, food-carrying water near the far shore. There are no insects hatching so I tie on one of my new caddis imitations dressed on a #14 hook. It's not that I expect a caddis hatch for hours, if then, but I choose this fly because its down-wing silhouette looks more like the houseflies, wasps, beetles, and stone flies that are the most likely windfalls than does the standard dry-fly silhouette. Then, too, it is the best floating fly in my box and this is pivotal.

I make my first cast twenty degrees downstream from straight across, curving my line so that it bellies upstream, landing the fly on the near edge of the deepish water. Within a second, I raise my rod tip sharply, making the fly lurch upstream an inch or so, then I feed out extra line so that the fly will float directly down-current. I keep my rod point high, to hold more line off the water for a truer float and also to absorb the shock of a strike, for the fish will hit against a tightening line.

Casting upstream to a fish in the classic manner. Line and leader may fall over fish. Downstream drag is a probability.

After six or eight feet of drag-free float, the fly will start to skitter across stream toward me and just as this motion starts a fish will often be goaded into taking. If no rise occurs after the fly has dragged a foot or so, I give a sharp tug on the line with my left hand to drown the fly and then snake it back upstream under the surface so that it won't frighten any nearby fish. My next cast is made eight feet farther across stream and is fished out in exactly the same manner — as is my third cast which is placed eight feet beyond the second. I have now covered the most likely holding water within easy reach with these three presentations so I wade to a position ten feet directly downstream, being careful not to send out advance-warning ripples, and prepare to make my next series of three covering casts. Depending on the size of the water, more or fewer casts may be needed to cover the lies thoroughly and this set of presentations should be repeated at ten-foot intervals all the way down to the tail of the pool or to a point where the water becomes too shallow to be worthwhile.

I have found that this method is not only vastly more productive than classic upstream prospecting, but that it is also far quicker. You can cover the best part of a pool of the size described above in about twenty minutes with this technique and then proceed to the vacant pool below with the assurance that you have covered more fish, and risen far more, than you could have in an hour and a half of conventional fishing.

One of the reasons for this is that a trout will move sideways five, even ten feet for a fluttering fly while a free-floater usually has to pass right over his nose to be effective. Then, too, the twitch pulls trout to the surface from far deeper water. Most flyfishers admit that it's hard to pound up fish with the floating fly in water over three feet deep unless spontaneous surface feeding is going on. Not so with the manipulated fly. It will trigger rises in six feet or more of water time and again — even under the noonday sun.

I'll have to admit, though, that I have drawn some flak from the establishment for angling this way. A couple of years ago, I was fishing behind a very proper older friend who stopped so long to

Casting to the same lie across and downstream. Fly approaches trout before the leader, and any drag is in upstream direction.

rest at a beautiful pool that I decided to pass him and push on upstream.

"Any luck?" I asked as I detoured behind him.

"Not a thing. Just look at that pool, though. It's got to be loaded, but I've been watching it for twenty minutes and I haven't seen so much as a dimple. I've had it. Why don't you show me how with that 'living insect' routine of yours?"

The water and the invitation were too good to pass up. I knotted on a caddis and started in at the top of the pool giving my high-floating fly a tiny twitch soon after it settled to the water.

Twenty minutes later, after I had raised seven trout, hooked five, and landed four good ones, I heard some heavy breathing close behind me.

"Very impressive. That popping bug of yours may well be the greatest invention since the worm."

My friend has since forgiven my fall from grace — somewhat. He will be seen with me in public, now, although he seems to duck me on the stream.

I look at it this way. I may have lost a fishing companion. But I have gained the companionship of a lot more trout. And, come to think of it, when I'm on the stream, that's the company I like best.

# 2

# The Alive-and-
# Kicking Dry Fly

If the evidence presented in the first chapter and a review of your own experiences have by now convinced you that a dry fly moved slightly and in the proper manner will outfish one that is presented absolutely dead drift, you may still have one lingering doubt. Why have so many seemingly intelligent men fished the standard floating fly drag-free for so long? After all, many leaders in business, science, and the arts (not to mention two of the last seven Presidents of the U.S.) have been dedicated flyfishers. Have they all been duped and deluded?

The answer, I think, lies somewhere between "Yes" and "Probably." And the reason such a thing could happen in this age of enlightenment makes a fascinating, though little-known, story.

Dry-fly fishing may have been developed over many years by many men, but it didn't reach the angling world at large until 1886. In that year, *Floating Flies and How to Dress Them* was published, and anglers haven't recovered from its enormous influence to this day. The author was Frederick M. Halford, an English gentleman, who gave up money-grubbing in all its forms at a relatively early age to devote his life to the nobler ideals of dry-fly fishing for trout.

The streams Halford fished are the most fertile in the world. The Test and Itchen in southern England produce twenty times as much trout food per cubic foot of water as do most famous streams on this side of the Atlantic. Back in Halford's fishing days, before road-washings, insecticides, and other pollutants had begun to take their toll, the hatches of insects, especially of mayflies, on these waters were incredibly profuse.

Under these conditions, a few fish rose fairly steadily all day long, and for several special hours every day when the glut hatches occurred, every fish in the river seemed to be on the take. It was a flyfisher's paradise and too perfect to be spoiled for other club members by some heavy-handed chap who put down the fish by flailing a team of wet flies through these clear waters in the hope of taking an unseen trout.

The accepted drill was quite specific. First a rising trout must be located. Then an accurate imitation of the fly on the water — not just some attractive and buggy-looking artificial—must be cast upstream of the trout and allowed to float, dead drift, over the nose of that particular fish. No attempt must be made to cater to its greed or curiosity. The only proper way to take such fish is to convince them that your counterfeit is, indeed, just another of the duns on which they have been feeding with confidence.

Fishermen on both sides of the Atlantic became fascinated by the science, skill, and delicacy of this new method. Halford became the high priest of a cult that spread the true doctrine with fanatical zeal. Soon the wet fly was considered a secret vice and club members caught using it were asked to resign their expensive rod privileges. The dry fly became a moral issue. After all, dammit, a gentleman didn't shoot grouse on the ground, he didn't cheat at cards, and he most certainly did not fish the wet fly, either!

From what I read, we seem to have shaken off most of our old Victorian hang-ups by this time, but the dry fly is still considered holier than the wet and the Halfordian dogma of dead drift seems to be a vestigial part of this ethical package. The moral origins of this doctrine may be lost in history, as far as most anglers are concerned, but the ritual is still with us.

In all fairness to Halford, though, I must repeat that he was fishing the stately chalkstreams of southern England which team with small mayflies. And, so even so, he included five highly realistic caddis patterns in his final selections of forty-three dry-fly patterns. But can we, who fish rivers that are mostly rain-fed, acid, and where caddis rival the mayflies for top place on the trout's menu, afford to ignore caddis imitations completely?

Rare photograph of Frederick M. Halford (left). "No wading" was his dictum, yet he is the only one wearing hip boots!

For we seem to be doing just that. For example, check the contents of your own dry-fly boxes. How many floating imitations of caddis flies do you carry? Don't count non-descripts or flies like the Adams which are said to duplicate some caddis but which are tied with the characteristic mayfly upwings and tails. I mean true caddis patterns like the English "sedges" with wings tied parallel to their bodies and which show a realistic caddis silhouette. Can you find many—or even any—in your fly boxes?

If you're like most anglers I know or meet—and many of these are advanced flyfishers — you probably don't have a single one. And chances are you can't find any at your favorite tackle shop, either. With the exception of a few terrestrials, nearly all floaters displayed in even the most fully stocked stores are designed to imitate some mayfly or other.

Admittedly, these popular mayfly patterns have proved themselves over and over again—*when there are enough mayflies hatching to start trout feeding regularly and selectively*. But how much of the time do you meet these conditions on the rivers you fish? What do you offer when caddis flies are hatching out in large numbers and trout are feeding on them selectively? What fly do you put on when stone flies are on the water? Or during those all-too-long periods when nothing is hatching and the trout are taking only the occasional, windfall, land-bred insects like bees, wasps, or houseflies? Is the traditional mayfly silhouette the most appealing to trout at times like these?

I think not. And I think this is the reason why the series of flies I have worked out to represent the most common species of caddis flies have proved themselves as excellent prospecting flies, too. Their silhouettes are more accurate representations of most land-bred windfall insects than are the shapes of the standard mayfly patterns.

Straw, ginger, brown, light dun, dark dun, and ginger-and-grizzly mixed have proved the most useful colors, but there are endless variations. Sizes 16 and 14 seem to cover most common caddis hatches, although I always carry some 18s and 12s just in case. Most of the caddis patterns I use have wings, hackle, and body of the same shade because caddis flies tend to be much the same color all over. My stone fly imitations, tied in the same manner, usually show more contrast, as do the naturals.

If you tie your own flies, or have a friend who ties for you, you may be interested in how these new Fluttering Caddis flies are tied. I start out by winding the tying silk back toward the tail, proceeding a little further than is customary, or just a bit around the bend. The reason for this is that most caddis have slightly down-pointing abdomens and because this fly needs more room at the eye-end of the hook. Tie in, at the point, two, at most three, strands of fine herl (pheasant-tail fibers are a good example) and very fine gold wire. Wind the herl up the shank, being careful to keep the body slim and even, to a point just halfway to the eye of the hook and fasten it down. The wire is then wound tightly to the same place with four or five even turns, but in an opposing spiral so that it binds down the herl and protects it.

Next comes the wing, and this must be put on with great care. Take a good spade feather, shoulder hackle, or the stiffest fibers on the neck that you usually reserve for tail materials, even up the points, and twitch off a section about three-fourths of an inch wide. Position this bunch on top of the hook so that from the tying-in point to tips it is about twice as long as the body, and bind it down with one full, firm turn of tying silk. If the fibers lie absolutely flat along the shank, you're in business. If not, take them off and build up the wingbed with thread until it is even with the hard portion of the herl body. When you have wound the body correctly with a suitable, small herl, this is seldom necessary, but these extra turns of silk can remedy any small error.

Once these top fibers are properly set, place two more bunches of the same bulk and length, one on each side of the hook, and tie them in with one turn each. Now half-hitch or weight the tying silk and examine the wing from all angles. When viewed from the rear, it should look like the upper half of a small tube, only slightly larger in diameter at the tail end than it is at the tying-in point. It should also veil the body a bit when viewed from the side. At this point you can still make minor adjustments by pinching and cajoling the fibers where they join the hook. Once you are satisfied with the overall appearance and symmetry, bind down firmly and finally with three or four turns of silk placed in tight sequence toward the head of the fly.

Take a fine, sharp pair of scissors and trim the wingbutts to form a gradual inclined plane, heaviest near the tying silk and coming to a point just back of the eye of the hook. It's a good idea to hold the wings firmly with your left thumb and forefinger right at the tying-in point while performing this delicate process so that the wing is not jostled out of position at this crucial stage. When the taper is absolutely even, take some varnish or cement and work it into the exposed butts to keep the slick hackle fibers from pulling out during the punishment of fishing. When the head becomes tacky, tie in two hackles of the usual size for that hook and wind them on in the conventional manner, being careful to bunch the turns tightly so they don't slide loosely down the inclined plane toward the eye of the hook. Whip finish, varnish the head, and the fly is finished.

Each caddis represents a larger-than-average investment in choice materials and in effort, but it's worth it in the long run. If properly tied, it will float higher and take more punishment than any other dry fly in your box. And, I've found, it will take more fish, too. Even if you're not a tyer, or don't know any, you should be able to give these new patterns a tryout next time you're on the stream, because several tackle companies now offer the caddis patterns in their catalogs.

I know this is not the perfect dry fly for every single situation, although I, myself, now use it the majority of the time. Of course, I still fish standard mayfly imitations when those naturals are on the water—though I often give even these easily sinkable patterns a tiny twitch when a steadily rising fish continues to ignore my artificial. I also know that this new method will never make me into the perfect flyfisherman, either. But with these patterns and this unorthodox presentation, I am now catching several times as many trout from hard-fished waters as I did a few years ago. Try them during a caddis or stone fly hatch or during those all-too-long "non-hatches." I think they'll do the same for you.

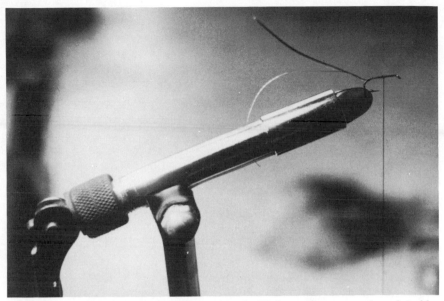

1. Herl and tinsel tied in at the bend. Tying silk returned and half-hitched slightly more than halfway up the hookshank.

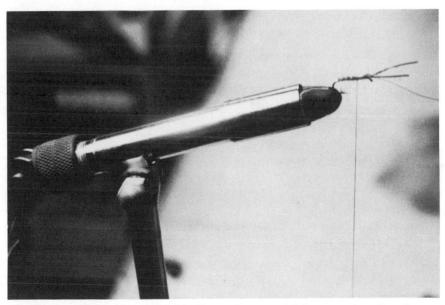

2. Body herl in place and binding wire wound in opposite direction. Keep body slim or wing will flair unnaturally.

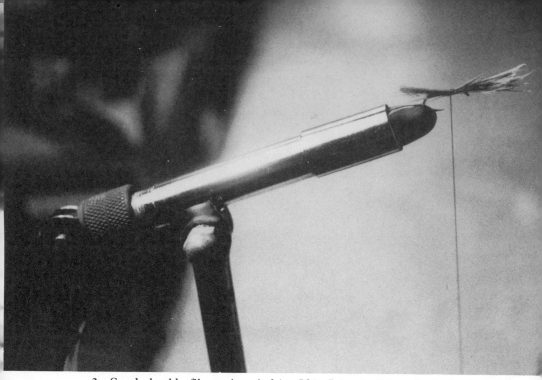

3. Spade-hackle fiber wing tied in. If it flairs, build up bed of tying silk ahead of body and seat it again.

4. Taper wing butts evenly to eye of hook and dose with varnish or cement. Hackle will not lie well on abrupt slope.

5. Two hackles of size appropriate to hook size tied in. Adding more tacky varnish or cement here is good insurance.

Hackle wound in close, even turns. Bunched hackle, small head, and flat wing enveloping body are signs of good work.

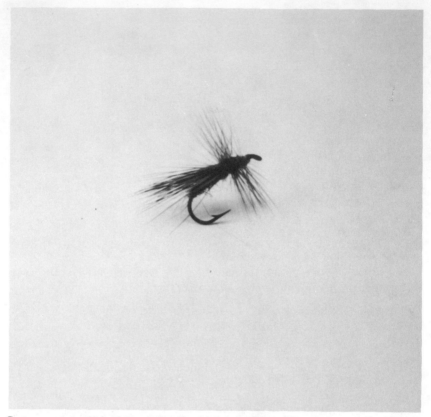

Same pattern tied with mink tail which is bulkier. The fly is equally killing, but less elegant in appearance.

# 3

# The Unsinkable Wet Fly

Most advanced flyfishermen I know seldom fish with wet flies anymore, and the youngest of them don't even carry wet-fly patterns. You don't have to be a research analyst to see that this has all the earmarks of a significant trend and, if it continues, in a few years it will be harder to find a wet fly than a #22 midge hook in a haystack. Today, nearly all sunk-fly fishing is done with nymphs. They've almost completely replaced the small, somber wet flies like the Leadwing Coachman, Hare's-Ear, and Dark Cahill, while the Mickey Finn, Muddler, and Spuddler seem to have shouldered the big, bright wets out of the fly hooks and into the attics where moths can complete their destruction.

This may or may not be a loss to fishermen, but fishing catalogs are certainly poorer because of it. Nothing dressed up a color plate as did the old Scarlet Ibis, Parmachene Belle, Silver Doctor, Jenny Lind, and their peer-group. Even our present-day salmon flies with their plain hair wings seem drab in comparison.

The reason these brilliant wet flies are no longer with us is that the special type of fishing for which they were designed disappeared long before they did. When the brook-trout ponds and lakes of Maine, the Adirondacks, and southern Canada were fished down, these patterns had no further purpose. But in their time and place they were murderous.

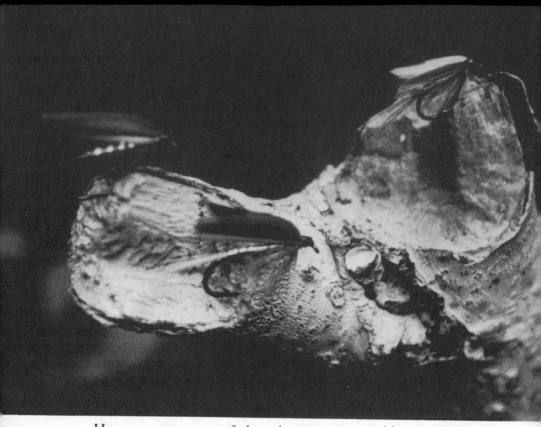

Have you seen any of these in recent years? Montreal (left), Silver Doctor (center), Parmachene Belle (right).

By sheer luck I caught the tail-end of this fishing many years ago in central New Brunswick, and if I hadn't experienced it myself I wouldn't believe the old-time stories. I had been staying at a salmon camp enjoying rotten fishing, and the operator, worried about the possible departure of his paying guests, came up with a delaying tactic. A new area had just been opened up by logging, he told us, and there was now a rough, but passable, road into an almost unfished lake. One logger who said he had fished there swore he'd had a hit on every cast.

We were not a gullible bunch but we were eight hundred miles from home with nothing better to do, so three of us made the trip in an old pickup truck over a road designed to make osteopaths rich. After we had arrived and were able to walk again we found the crude raft the logger had made and drifted out onto the lake. And for once everything we'd been told by an outfitter was absolutely true.

Very soon, the promised hit on every cast became monotonous, so we started experimenting. Two flies? Doubles. Three flies?

Triples. Then the one man who'd stuck with the single fly said excitedly, "Even when I've got a fish on, I'm still getting hits. I'll bet they're striking the leader knots." After he landed the fish he tied a couple of small bare hooks in at the knots of this gut leader and cast out again. He'd guessed right; he landed his first triple.

One thing we all noticed that day was the brighter the fly, the faster the hit and the bigger the trout. One member of the party found a few old Parmachene Belles in his vest and these were the best of all. They accounted for nearly all the big fish—those of a pound or better—while smaller, duller flies caught nothing over ten inches. The reason was simple. The more successful fish, the ones that had grown big, were the fish that won the race to the food, no matter what it looked like, and it paid to advertise your hook to them. Caution and delicate presentation had nothing to do with success on these virgin waters. Here the old bright wet flies on hulking #6 hooks were supreme.

The Muddler Minnow (top) and the Mickey Finn, two attractor flies that have replaced gaudy wets for pounding up fish.

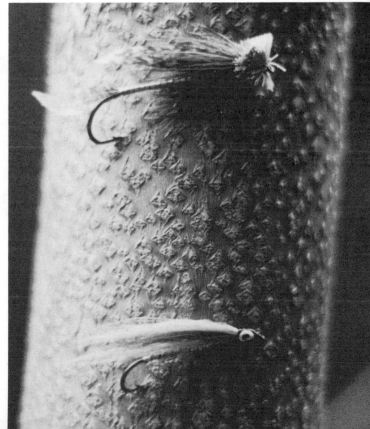

The good old days, when baskets of big trout were expected. Believe it or not, fish once fought each other for the fly.

Though these flashy wet flies had lost their effectiveness on most ponds and lakes long before my day, some of the more subdued patterns from the same generation are still worth carrying. The Black Gnat is a fine imitation of a big housefly or black land beetle. The White Miller can't be equaled when white caddis are hatching out on a Northern lake. The Grizzley King is a useful imitation of many green-bodied caddis flies, and the Montreal duplicates some of the darker species in this order of insects.

When flies like these were arbitrarily discarded along with the Christmas-tree wilderness flies, the baby may have been thrown out with the bathwater. There's a lot about the shape and style of the old wet fly to recommend it—so much that I'm working on a whole series of flies based on this principle.

The emphasis on more accurate imitation, the very movement that brought in the nymph as a replacement for the old wet fly, is responsible for leading me in this direction. The patterns I've come up with so far are different from the old ones, but more in color than in shape. When more anglers and fly-tyers turn their attention to the neglected wet fly I'm sure that even the few classic patterns that have survived the nymphing revolution will be redesigned or replaced.

One of these that is still popular in the East is the wet version of the Quill Gordon, which is carried and used by many who consider themselves exact imitationists. Since many books have told us that this mayfly (*Epeorus pleuralis*) leaves its nymphal shuck on the river floor and ascends through the water to the surface as a winged adult, a wet-fly pattern is the logical choice until, of course, the fish become preoccupied with surface feeding on the fully-formed adults. But which wet fly? The Quill Gordon?

This pattern has yellow wings, a black-and-white striped body, and dun-colored legs. The natural fly is distinctly different, with dark dun wings, creamy-olive body, and dark brown mottled legs. The old English Greenwell pattern, with a slight alteration in the body, is the best imitation I've ever seen or tried. I've fished my version of this fly as part of a two-fly team along with the standard Quill Gordon, altering their positions on the leader regularly, and over the past thirteen springs it has outfished the wet Gordon better than two to one.

The real nymph-maniacs prefer the grey-colored Quill Gordon nymph which tackle suppliers are all too eager to sell you. I wonder why this pattern appears in so many catalogs. The nymph never rises to the surface, as we have noted, and it is one of the last nymphs to be dislodged by high water. It is a fast-water dweller with a short, flattened body and will only be swept away when the rock or boulder it's hiding under gets rolled over by the force of a flood. Long before this occurs the trout will have gorged themselves on the less-secure nymphs washed down to them. I doubt that Quill Gordon nymphs ever lose their grip until the river is so high and muddy that any sort of fly-fishing is impossible. This may be a useful general pattern, but I don't think trout mistake it for the Quill Gordon nymph.

The Quill Gordon, both the artificial and the natural, is an extremely popular and famous fly that has been observed and studied more than most. But how many other mayflies emerge in the same manner and would be better imitated by a wet-fly pattern than by a nymph? And how many caddis flies and stone flies are there that share this underwater emerging behavior? Entomology doesn't provide many answers—aquatic insects haven't been given much attention by scientists lately—but my guess is that this type of emergence is a lot more common than we realize. Remember, the wet fly was not invented in America to catch ravenous and overpopulated brook trout. The silhouette and the style were worked out in England over several centuries to catch sophisticated and finicky brown trout.

There's another part of the life-cycle of aquatic insects that is ignored by the angler who limits himself to dry flies and nymphs exclusively. What happens to flies after they die? The great majority of them fall on the water, of course, which explains why fishing with mayfly-spinner imitations is so effective at dusk. But what about the spent flies—mayflies, caddis flies, and stone flies—that aren't taken in the pool where they fall but get churned underwater in the rapids directly below? Could a dry fly or nymph imitate these soggy, but winged, insects as well as the

The Quill Gordon wet fly (right) and the modified Greenwell, which is a better duplicate of the emerging natural.

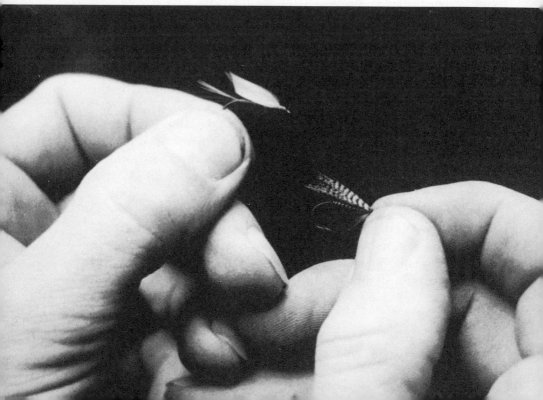

classic wet fly in some pattern or form? I am fully convinced that many early and successful wet flies were winged with pale starling primary feathers to imitate mayfly spinners that had gone down for the third time and had been swept downriver for the waiting fish.

The much-neglected caddis flies may give us even more reasons to reconsider the old wet fly. Some common species seem to spring fully fledged from the water as if they had escaped from their pupal shucks well below the surface. Have they hatched directly out of their cases on the stream-bottom the way the Quill Gordon mayflies do? I'm betting on it. And don't some other species, with their seemingly instantaneous hatch-out on the surface, appear more like winged adults than pupae as they make this hazardous trip? I'm sure this is the case with many common species. And yet all the new patterns of emerging caddis I see in tackle stores and catalogs are slavish imitations of the pupae as they appear when they are hauled dormant from their cases.

Another caddis behavior pattern that recommends a wet-fly imitation is the egg-laying of several species. Did you know that some (we don't know exactly how many) crawl down roots, rocks, twigs or weed stalks to lay their eggs underwater? When these have deposited their eggs and drift down-current, dying, the wet fly has to be the most killing imitation.

It is interesting to note that fishermen who have witnessed this egg-laying technique say that the mature female insect takes a bubble of air underwater with her and that she appears like a moving drop of silver. Modern flyfishermen who wouldn't be caught dead fishing a wet fly sporting a tag or entire body of tinsel have, perhaps, outsmarted themselves.

There's another reason to reevaluate the old tinsel-bodied wet fly. We know that a bubble of gas develops rapidly under the pupal shuck of caddis flies and under the nymphal skin of mayflies just before they emerge. The gas bubble helps them hatch out. How does this make the insect appear to the trout? Is the exact color of a nymph or pupa—examined hours or days before it heads for the surface—what the trout sees during this critical time when the insects are most available as food? Or is there a very different silver or golden flash caused by this gas bubble in emergers that telegraphs to the trout that this is their

The big, bright, brook-trout flies of yesteryear. Tackle catalogs haven't looked the same since trout became scarce.

target of the moment? I am not convinced that modern fly-tying isn't presenting a whole series of death-mask flies to trout. A lot of observation and experimentation is in order here before we completely abandon flies that have served fishermen so well for centuries.

Every year or so now a new series of nymphs is presented to fishermen, and each is highly acclaimed because it appears to our eyes even more faithful to the naturals than the previous attempts. The last group of imitations I saw had the precise number of tails (or setae) the naturals have, and six perfectly formed legs with the correct number of joints in each leg. They were every bit as realistic as the figures in Mme. Tussaud's waxworks. And, like those famous statues, they were also as stiff as boards because their realism had been achieved by stiffening the appendages of the flies with lacquer.

Flies like these deserve to be carefully mounted and exhibited, but it would be almost sacrilegious to fish with them. It might also be a waste of time. A few years ago there were many nymphs made of molded plastic that looked as if they could crawl out of their fly-box compartments, and yet they were indifferent fish-takers and have nearly disappeared from the market. The short-coming was that they, and many of the newer patterns formed with lacquered feathers, were designed from models that were the preserved corpses of nymphs. Have you ever watched a living mayfly nymph or stone fly larva underwater? The gills appear enormous, are fluttering constantly, and are very often quite different in color from the body of the insect.

There's a lot of evidence that the motion of these gills and the scampering movement of the legs identify these nymphs as living food to the trout, and that the precise color and size, though important, are secondary. Any stiff, lacquered imitation loses this seductive quality of movement and much of the natural insect's translucence as well. I admire these new photographically realistic nymphs as art forms, but they leave me lukewarm as lures for trout.

Perhaps the most compelling case of all for the old wet fly is that it moved and breathed with every subtle change in current. Wet flies, as we have noted, were probably designed to imitate many life-phases of many types of insects, yet they can perform splendidly as imitations of mayfly nymphs when specifically tied for this purpose. The wet versions of the Light Cahill and March Brown, for example, with their darker, striped topsides, can be deadly imitations when the corresponding nymphs are hatching out. The secret here is to tie the wings in low and on the sides, as you would with a strip-wing salmon fly, so that they hug the top half of the body. Their silhouette is then sleek and nymphlike, yet there's still an extra "aliveness" to the play in the wing-fibers that the standard nymph-dressing can't equal.

I have a whole series of wet flies like these—different from the ones duplicating emerging or drowned flies — and I have more confidence in them than I have in the popular nymph-dressings of the same insects. I'll admit I haven't tested these against the standard nymphs, two on a leader, the way I have the wet Quill Gordon, so I can't quote any catch figures. However, everything I've learned about trout and trout-fly tying, as well as my results, convince me that I'm on to a more productive style of fly.

To increase the breathing, moving characteristics of these patterns, I pluck out a lot of body dubbing with a needle or substitute ostrich herl dyed to an exact color for the body material. This increases the fly's similarity to a living nymph with its fluttering gills, and I'm sure this adaptation will increase the effectiveness of most nymph patterns, too.

I came upon this trick, which is certainly not original, after many years of learning the hard way. I didn't jump to this conclusion easily after hearing all those stories about the chewed-up, tattered fly outfishing all others, although it is now one of the few pieces of fishing folklore I firmly believe. No, I had to be taught this lesson, piece by piece, by a kindly but self-serving expert.

Early in my fly-fishing career and before I tied my own flies, I often fished with an elderly gentleman who appeared to be uncommonly generous. He would press on me all sorts of wet-fly and nymph patterns during a day's fishing, and since good flies cost the princely price of a quarter apiece in those days, I looked upon him as a walking gold mine. However, at the end of each day's efforts he questioned me about the performance of each of the donated flies, and graciously accepted the slightly used artificials back into his own box. With my usual hawkeyed hindsight, I'm

now convinced that the old bandit wasn't the least bit interested in
my researches; he knew exactly what he was doing. He was using
me to "warm up" his flies for him, to get them into shaggy,
fish-catching shape while he used the ones that were already in
vintage condition. It turned out to be the classic case of one hand
washing the other. My weekly allowance was minute and his fly
supply was almost infinite.

Imitation of some sort or other is probably the key to success
with today's hard-pounded trout. But what sort of imitation? You
can imitate an insect's overall behavior pattern, for instance. You
can also imitate the small motions of its gills, tails, legs, and
antennae. Or you can imitate its color, shape, and appendages
down to the minutest detail. I doubt, however, that any single
nymph dressing can excel at all three types of duplication. You
have to compromise somewhere and, with nymphs, I prefer to
skimp on exact anatomical details. I feel my more alive patterns
perform at least as well as the more static, more photographic,

Wet fly imitating the March Brown nymph or emerger. Notice how
mallard-flank wing hugs ostrich-herl body.

dressings when matching a specific emerging nymph, and that when I use them for random prospecting they are far superior.

The wet flies I use to represent winged emergers, drowned adults, and egg-layers seem to be without any major shortcomings. Wings and legs are responsive and mobile without sacrifice of true-to-life detail. I can't fault them in accuracy, theory, or performance.

I think the easiest and most convincing type of wet-fly fishing, if you want to take it up or try it again, can be experienced at the end of a summer evening. Until the light gets too dim to see your fly on the water, fish the dry-spinner imitation of the spent mayfly you've seen fall to the water, and fish it dead drift. Then, for the last fly of the day, tie on a standard wet fly of the same size and color. Go downstream a short distance to the head of the pool below where the current begins to lose its chop, and cast your fly straight across stream, letting it swim till it comes to a stop directly below you. Repeat at one-step intervals until the water gets too slow to pull your fly through the arc in a satisfactory manner.

Feel your way carefully downstream with your feet, but be sure to feel your line and rod with equal sensitivity. You should get some thumping strikes and — if you don't strike back too quickly as I usually do—some exciting fish. If you're like me, you'll probably find that the night is absolutely black before you decide it's time to stop.

Even the most fastidious flyfisher should feel happy after this type of angling, for he has been an exact imitationist the entire time. This is not chuck-and-chance-it with a nondescript. He has been presenting the closest possible imitation of the fly of the moment to the fish in exactly the same manner in which the naturals are coming to them. Most important of all, at a time of day when he is likely to be bone-tired, the angler has not had to strain his eyes, strike on hunches, or worry about whether or not his fly is still floating.

If this experiment in wet-fly fishing convinces you there's something here, perhaps you'll tie and try the wet fly on other occasions, too. Not as a mere blob of food, but as an imitation of a specific life-stage of an identified insect. If you keep an open mind and compare results with fishing companions, I think you'll find the drill exciting and rewarding. You won't be exploring a new frontier, but you will be adding a third dimension to your dry-fly/nymph style of trout fishing, and, when you start observing flies and fly behavior for yourself without relying on some other man's word, you'll find a whole new and productive world of fishing.

Every year sunk-fly men seem to add more weight to their flies, leaders, or lines to make sure their nymphs bump along the very bottom of the stream. No doubt this has made fly-fishing more effective—especially when the trout aren't feeding. But it has also made casting and fishing less pleasant. So much so that many anglers will spin or bait-fish rather than torture their rods and their arms in this manner.

The wet-fly fishing I'm practicing and proposing takes a middle ground and covers the middle depth of the water. Here you don't need sashweights or heavy lead-core lines because emergers, egg-layers, and drowned flies don't hug the bottom the way nymphs do. They're not far under the surface, and you can present their counterfeits realistically with regular tackle and a floating line. Surprisingly often, this is exactly what the trout ordered.

It seems that fly-fishing becomes more complicated and technical every year, and perhaps this is necessary to achieve best results under demanding circumstances. But shouldn't fly-fishing be a joy as well as a challenge? Men in less harried times certainly thought so. They fished the wet fly with grace and pleasure, not feeling that every fish in the stream had to be yanked out of it. The surprising thought is that they just may have been using the most effective imitation of all.

# 4

## Give Summer Trout a Moveable Feast

The average dry-fly fisherman is about as well equipped to fool summer trout as a golfer would be to win the Masters with a bag full of putters. For in any sport you're handicapped when you limit yourself to just one aspect of the game.

All those patterns, sizes, and colors you see in a fly box don't mean real variety to a trout. Most of the flies will be the same shape. The reason for this is that over ninety-nine percent of the dry flies sold today—from minute midges to galumphing #8s—have an identical silhouette. Their sweeping tails, slim bodies and upright wings show they're an imitation of some type of mayfly and, unfortunately, mayflies are only an occasional snack for summer trout.

Most of our dry-fly patterns have been handed down to us from happier days on insect-rich streams where mayflies were, indeed, the major source of insect food. Our most popular dries are direct descendants of mayfly imitations worked out by Frederick Halford on England's prolific chalkstreams nearly a century ago. We still slavishly cast these imitations to our trout, despite the fact that entomologists — and the proof-positive stomach contents of our trout — tell us that trout in America today make far more meals on the three other orders of insects that hatch off the water and on random, land-bred insects than they do on Halford's hallowed mayflies. In light of this, casting a repertoire consisting of artificial mayflies only is about as realistic as Marie Antoinette's advice for the starving peasants: "Let them eat cake."

Similarly, the dead-drift, upstream presentation preached by Halford is a relic from the good old days, too. An accurate imitation of a natural fly fished in a free-floating manner may still work—and work well—when trout are rising regularly to a particular species of fly. But what about all those hours when trout aren't actively feeding? Will a totally unexpected fly with some fifty extra legs, too many tails, and a great hook hanging down below it seem real enough to pull a wary trout up off the bottom? Or will he class it with the twigs, berries, hemlock needles, and leaf cuttings that also drift over his lie all day long? The latter is usually the case as most of us know from sad experience. Under these conditions, your imitation needs something extra going for it if you are to convince the trout that your counterfeit is, indeed, alive.

To catch a loafing trout's attention and to gain his confidence, your dry fly should move—and move as a living insect does. This means a small movement, not a great plowing wake. And it should move in an *upstream* direction. For all stream-bred flies, whether hatching out or returning for egg-laying, move in an up-current direction.

The reason the moving dry fly has been damned for decades is not that natural flies don't move, but that when the fisherman cast his fly up-current—as doctrine dictated—any motion except for a free drift was either downstream, across-stream, or both . . . behavior patterns so unrealistic and alarming that they send all but the most calloused trout scurrying for cover.

If, on the other hand, you break with tradition and cast your fly in an across-and-downstream direction, when you give it a tiny twitch it will lurch upstream. Then let it float free again as long as it will. That small motion is enough to catch the trout's attention and tell him that your offering is, indeed, alive and edible. Gently does it, though. The game is like calling ducks. Overdo it and you defeat your own ends.

This slightly moved dry fly is the only way I've ever been able to raise trout consistently when they're slightly lethargic during the summer months and there are no big fly hatches to keep them

feeding regularly on the surface. This method will even raise good
fish out of a deep slow water at midday when only mad dogs and
Englishmen would think of being astream.

There's just one problem with this seemingly unorthodox system. You probably haven't a fly in your box that will keep
floating—and floating high—after you've given it that tantalizing
twitch. Then, too, the mayfly silhouette—even if this type of fly
occasionally remained afloat—doesn't look like most midsummer
insects. It has long tails, is basically translucent, and has upright
wings. The other important insects that emerge from the water—
caddis flies, stone flies, true flies, and nearly all insects that are
blown onto the water from the neighboring land—have no tails or
very small ones, wings that lie along the top or sides of the body
and are basically opaque.

Cut open the next trout you catch on a midsummer afternoon
(if you can take one on a standard fly) and examine the stomach
contents carefully. I'm sure that what you'll find there would
make Halford whirl in his grave like a #10 fanwing cast on a
gossamer 8X tippet. Ants, wasps, bees, crane flies, beetles, and
houseflies will form the bulk and, if there are any aquatic insects
in the mix, there will probably be as many caddis flies and stone
flies as there are mayflies. If you'll take a trout stomach's word for
what he's been eating, you'll have to ask yourself the agonizing
question: "What do I match when there's no hatch?"

And this is a question you'll have to answer for a greater part of
the day over a longer portion of the season in the years ahead. For
good hatches of mayflies are disappearing on most of our waters.
They are already a great rarity on most northeastern waters after
June 1, and really profuse early-season hatches are becoming
infrequent enough to be talked about again and again as major
events.

Caddis hatches, on the other hand, seem to be as heavy as ever
and stone flies, the third most important order of aquatic insects,
seem to be holding their own, too. Apparently, both of these
types of insects are tougher and more tolerant of the flooding,
heating, and polluting that progress brings to our running waters.

Yet perhaps the most important part of the trout's diet during
mid and late summer is made up of the wide variety of land-bred

insects that fall onto the water. Grasshoppers and beetles have long been recognized as trout delicacies, and good imitations are available at many tackle stores. But what about the other windfalls that trout feed on during hot weather?

The observant fishermen in Pennsylvania's limestone country have come up with ingenious imitations of the leaf-hoppers, Japanese beetles, and tiny ants that fall onto their waters. But little attention has been paid to the corresponding insects that tumble into woodland streams at this time of year. Terrestrial insects are equally important to mountain trout as they are to fish inhabiting meadow streams flowing through rich agricultural areas, but they are a very different looking collection.

In an attempt to fill this important, though empty, corner of our fly boxes, I have experimented with a series of prototypes that cover most of the insects I find on mountain streams and inside trout during midsummer. You should certainly enlarge on and vary this selection by copying insect types you find most frequently in your area. All these flies, despite their apparent differences in size, shape, and color, have one characteristic in common. They are the most buoyant artificials I have ever fished with. They will ride high and cocky on the surface even after they have been twitched smartly.

These imitations are no more difficult to tie than standard patterns, but there are a few tricks that may make your first attempts easier. This series of flies, for tying purposes, can be separated into three broad types that are different in small, though important ways.

The tying of caddis imitations was treated earlier in Chapter 2. Stone fly imitations are made in much the same way except for slight variations in both the body and the wing. Stone fly bodies should be more succulent, should be colored yellow, brown, or an alternating pattern of the two. Ostrich herl is a good choice here since it gives a chunky appearance without adding much real bulk. This wing, too, should be twice the body length and placed on top of the hook only instead of on top and along the sides. Use light grey or pale dun hackle since these are the usual stone fly wing colors. Hackle at the head should be the same size as you would use for the caddis and wound on in the same

A dry stone-fly artificial on long-shank hook with ostrich-herl body. Hackle-fiber wing hugs top of body.

Top view of dry crane-fly imitation. Outrigger wings of dun-hackle fibers recreate flair of natural's wings.

A flying black-ant pattern seen from above. Ant wings also flair to the side away from distinctive body silhouette.

Side view of floating bumblebee. Body is formed of alternating black and yellow ostrich herl. Outrigger wings on side.

manner, but choose a shade that matches the body rather than the wing color. The above suggestions cover the great majority of stone flies you'll see on mountain streams, but by all means imitate any other color combinations you see regularly on the streams you fish.

Crane flies, houseflies, wasps, bees, and flying ants are the easiest of all to tie. Start with a good, meaty body, colored to match the species in question. You won't have to stint here because you'll want the wings to flair on these flies. Here again use pale dun or grizzly hackle fibers, keeping them the same length as before, but positioning them on the sides of the hook shank only. The finished wings should flair out to the sides at an angle of about thirty degrees the way a bee's or housefly's wings do. These outriggers of steely hackle will not only make your fly ride high but will help it sit squarely, hook down, every time you cast it. Finish these flies as you did the stone fly imitations, with two conventional hackles suggesting body color rather than wing color.

These summer flies will float twice as well as standard mayfly imitations if you tie them with the same quality of hackle. The only trouble is that you'll be using a lot more long-fibered hackle which is often hard to get in first-rate quality. Substitute hair whenever you can get good water-repellant guard-hairs of the right color. Mink tail is excellent and is produced by breeders in a wide variety of shades. Beaver gives a good dark brown. Woodchuck tail — even though the animal isn't aquatic — sheds water beautifully. So does moose mane. Be careful with deer tail, though. Some portions are useful, but most of it is hollow and will flair badly when tied to the hook.

Admittedly, these patterns are not exact imitations of the flies you'll find in midsummer trout. But they are very appealing *impressions* of these windfall insects, and fish aren't highly selective at this time of year because they don't often see large enough quantities of the same insect to get psychologically imprinted with an exact size, shape, and color. The trick is to give them the *sort* of fly they've been taking and to present it as a struggling, but sitting, duck.

On some afternoons one fly will be preferred; on others a different one will pull more trout to the surface. Experiment. But be guided in your first choice by what you see in the air and on the water. Crane flies often hover and dance over the surface, and an imitation can be deadly when you see a few yo-yoing over a pool. Always be on the alert for a flight of ants—especially when the weather is hot and sunny.

You may wonder why I tie my flying-ant imitations in this manner since it is well known that these insects usually ride flush in the surface film, rather than high and dry like stream-bred insects. The answer is that, when flying ants fall on the water during midsummer afternoons, they are liable to be so numerous that your artificial stands a fractional chance of being taken unless it advertises itself as a newcomer by its activity. A standard ant can't take the twitch and remain floating while this pattern can. I've found that the twitched imitation will outfish the low-riding, dead-drift one by a wide margin — especially when there are a dozen or more ants per square foot of water.

Above all, when you're prospecting with these flies on a midsummer morning or afternoon, spray or anoint your fly liberally and change it at the first hint of sogginess. In this type of fishing a half-drowned fly is as much use as wet matches.

Why do I continue to fish the dry fly during the dog days—and hours—when nothing seems to be rising? Why don't I turn to the upstream, dead-drift nymph that so many authors recommend for these conditions? There are three reasons, and any single one of them would be enough to keep me fishing on the surface.

First, upstream nymphing is the most demanding and least diverting kind of trout fishing I've ever tried. It takes far more judgment and concentration to fish an unseen nymph up-current without any drag than it does to fish the dry fly in this manner. There's no visible fly to help you regulate your rate of retrieve or to tell you when to strike, either. I find this technique cruel and unusual punishment unless the fish are taking readily. A half-hour without a hit is the outside limit of my attention span.

Second, I think it's harder to deceive a trout with a nymph than it is with a dry fly. A floating fly has to be glimpsed through the distorting prisms that hackle fibers set up in the surface tension giving the trout a blurred view. A nymph, on the other hand, is seen directly through the clear water and any imperfections stand out sharply—probably the reason why wet flies and nymphs work best only in fast or turbulent currents.

But the third, and main, reason that the dry fly, properly fished, will beat the sunk fly under low water conditions is that the surface carries most of the insect food at this time of year. The stream-bed may be teeming with nymphs, but they hide under rocks during the day and crawl out only at dusk or after dark. Summertime aquatic insects rarely swim up to emerge till late evening and even then they may be pitifully few in number. The main food supply most of the day is made up of insects that have flown or tumbled onto the surface and these, trapped in the rubbery surface film, are carried downstream on top of the water. Sample the drift food in a stream at this time of year with a cheesecloth net and you'll find that the middle and lower layers of the current yield almost no food at all.

For all of these reasons, then, you can presume that daytime feeding fish are expecting their food on the surface. This is fortunate for the angler, for here his fly stands the best chance of both catching the fish's attention and preventing him from getting too close a look at the imitation.

This type of floating fly fished with motion not only helps you catch more trout, but it lets you catch them out of more parts of the stream or river. With this technique in hand, you won't have to compete with other anglers at the heads of pools or along the few fast runs. A fly twitched slightly on the surface will raise trout all day long on the much-neglected pools and long flats where the dead-drift nymph or dry fly would seem very dead, indeed.

Equally important, this method will help you catch fish during more of the daylight hours. You will no longer have to pin all your hopes on that last-minute flurry of feeding as darkness ends the summer day. If you have a several-hour round-trip drive to your favorite stream — as most of us do — this benefit alone is enough to make this technique worth cultivating.

I hold no brief for quoting scripture loosely just to prove your case, but I can't resist pointing out that the Old Testament Book of Proverbs advises "Go to the ant, thou sluggard . . ." I think all flyfishermen will agree that before editing and translating the line must have read, "Go to the ant, wasp, bee, beetle, crane fly, housefly," and so on. After all, the Holy Land is warm-weather territory. And from where else would you expect such good advice on how to catch fish when the rivers are low and sluggardly?

# 5

## *Izaak Who?*

We all know that fame is a fickle thing at best, yet when it comes to angling laurels we have the crowning irony. Not one person in a hundred has ever heard of Frederick Halford or Theodore Gordon—flyfishermen whose pioneering changed the way millions of people fish today—while every man, woman, and child seems to know the name of that unrepentant baitslinger and wormfisherman, Izaak Walton.

It's not that I'm judging the man on the basis of what he put on his hook. I'm no archpurist and I've wet a worm or two, or worse, in my day. The reason I find Walton's immortality a mockery is the fact that the man was a plagiarist.

Now don't start reaching for your well-thumbed copies of Krafft-Ebing or Havelock Ellis because I'm not accusing Walton of some unmentionable and degenerate deviation. A plagiarist, as any Ph.D. in English literature well knows, is simply a literary thief, and on this count Walton was as guilty as sin.

The literary critics and English professors of the world, to whom Walton had always been a darling, were badly shaken up on the morning of December 17, 1956. On that day, a front-page article in no less than The New York *Times* headlined, "Did Walton Hook 'Angler' From Older Book?" exposed the original, and long-lost, source from which much of Walton's classic had been, shall we say, borrowed.

This news item described a book called *The Arte of Angling*, printed in London in 1577, that had recently been found in the attic of an old English country home. It consisted of a dialogue between Viator and Piscator, the same two characters we find in Walton's book. The general narrative line and structure of the two books were surprisingly similar, the experts noted, and several passages were almost word for word the same. Coincidence? Two great minds working alike? Little chance of that, said the learned men who were analyzing the new find. *The Arte* had been published eighty years before Walton's book, or well before Izaak had been born.

This exposé and its implications did not go unchallenged. The very next day a short item on the Walton affair appeared in the middle of the *Times* with a defense of Walton by D. E. Rhodes, a British expert on early fishing classics. "It seems to me unjust," said this authority, "to accuse Izaak Walton of plagiarism, because plagiarism did not exist in the seventeenth century. All authors in that and earlier ages read what they liked and used what they liked without acknowledgment." True, perhaps, but I am not swayed. Monarchs, in those days, frequently and quite legally chopped off the heads of those who disagreed with them, but the fact that this was no crime does not convince me that head-chopping-off is a blameless form of recreation. (Furthermore, as we shall see in a moment, one of Walton's own contemporaries considered word-larceny a vulgar enough offense to be labeled a "common calamity," and he forthwith accused Walton of "Plagiary.")

A few smaller stories and mentions appeared in the press over the next month or so, and then the whole issue became history. Walton's reputation remained untarnished.

Why wasn't Walton discredited and defrocked by the literary pundits? It wasn't as if some new Dead Sea Scroll had been found showing that St. Peter had actually been in the wholesale fish business and had never caught a fish in his life. St. Peter is a towering figure in both history and religion, and fishermen are justly proud that their patron saint is one of the most important of all.

But Walton . . . who sanctified him? He is of very little interest to contemporary fishermen and owes most of his fame to the fact that his book is required reading in many English literature courses. Were the implications of this revelation too uncomfortable to the academic establishment of Walton-worshippers? Was Walton too small a fish in the literary swim to merit a major Shakespeare-Bacon controversy? Was the word "Walton" too indispensable to journalists as a synonym after they had used up "fisherman" and "angler"? Did the Izaak Walton League exert its influence to clamp a lid on the story? Nobody has yet come up with an explanation.

Equally hard to understand is the fact that the scholars were taken by surprise when this new evidence emerged. Actually, Walton had been caught out very early in the game. His contemporary, Richard Frank, whose *Northern Memoirs* came out in 1658, just five years after the first printing of *The Compleat Angler*, called out "foul" loud and clear: "He stuffs his Book with Morals from Dubravius and others, not giving us one Precedent of his own practical Experiments, except otherwise where he prefers the Trencher before the Troling-rod; who lays the stress of his Arguments upon other Men's Observations, wherewith he stuffs his indigested *Octavo*; so brings himself under the Angler's Censure, and the common Calamity of a Plagiary, to be pitied (poor Man) for his loss of time, in scribbling and transcribing other Men's Notions."

Walton may or may not have been a great stylist, but Frank could wield words with the best of them. He winds up the above indictment of Walton and his kind with ringing words: "These be the drones that rob the hive yet flatter the bees they bring them honey." Didn't anyone read, or listen to, Frank?

Elsewhere in *Northern Memoirs* Frank describes a face-to-face argument he once had with Izaak, and we get more clues to Walton's original sources. Walton took the position that pickerel were generated from pickerel weed while Frank claimed that they were born from eggs laid by their parents, like every other fish. Walton cited his authorities for this point — Gesner, Dubravius (there's that man again), and Androvanus—and, when pressed by Frank, refused to discuss the matter further and walked off in a huff.

We have always known that Walton was a rotten speller, but this incident reveals that he was also woefully misinformed about the habits of fish — even for his own time. Again we find him borrowing from outdated authorities. One of them, Dubravius, was mentioned specifically in Frank's earlier accusation of outright theft, but had Walton also cribbed from the other two to fill his book? And is the author of *The Arte of Angling* yet another source, unknown to Frank, that Walton may have dipped into? We may never know. The first three pages — including the title page — of that recently discovered work were missing and there isn't another copy anywhere.

One of the commonest tributes paid to Walton's book is the serenity and tranquility of the work even though it was written during Britain's bitter Civil War. This is often cited as proof of the beauty of Walton's soul. I hope we don't hear that argument anymore. It appears certain that the original had been conceived back in the rollicking days of good Queen Bess.

As a matter of fact, *The Compleat Angler* has never been very popular reading with fishermen — at least not Walton's portion of it. Walton was more concerned with how to prepare baits, cook fish, and watch milkmaids than he was with fly-fishing. The raising and care of maggots and the kneeding of exotic paste-baits to entice overgrown, vegetarian minnows haven't fascinated anglers for many years. Most of the passages quoted by fishing authors are from Part II, written for later editions by Charles Cotton. This prompted the late Eric Taverner, one of the finest fishing writers of our century, to say, "Walton without Cotton is like good manners without meat." A little-known fact is that the fly-fishing sections of the earlier editions were contributed by an expert cook named Thomas Barker who was also a fine fishing writer in his own right.

Walton has not always received universal acclaim. Several non-fishing writers of note have taken issue with Walton on other grounds. Leigh Hunt labeled him a "worm-sticker" and went on to find fault with his face as well. "It is hard, angular, and of no expression. It seems to have been 'subdued to what it worked in'; to have become native to the watery element. One might have said to Walton, 'Oh, flesh, how art thou fishified!' He looks like a pike dressed in broadcloth instead of butter."

Lord Byron was even less generous, calling him a "sentimental savage whom it is the mode to quote (amongst novelists) to show

Izaak Walton lived to a ripe old age—as this portrait
by Jacob Huysman proves. Did his conscience ever
bother him?

their sympathy for innocent sports and old songs, who teaches
how to sew up frogs and break their legs by way of
experiment. . . ." Byron goes on to cap his condemnation with a
bit of doggerel:

> The quaint, old, cruel coxcomb, in his gullet
> should have a hook, and a small trout to pull it.

While it is interesting to note that writers were quoting Walton
over 150 years ago to show how with-it they were in an outdoorsy
way, the influence of Walton has had another, more pernicious

Charles Cotton by Sir Peter Lely. Without Cotton's contributions, *The Compleat Angler* would never have been compleat.

effect: It has ruined more fishing writing than any other single cause. The entire time-honored "cutesy-poo" school of outdoor writing is directly descended from *The Compleat Angler*.

Ever since that book was first acclaimed as a classic because of its scope and style, other fishing writers have tried to follow in the great man's footsteps. They have wanted it understood that they, too, were beautiful, sensitive people who had discovered deeper truths through fishing and other pastoral pursuits.

This type of prose is the high-wire act of the writing business. You have no facts, no characters, no suspense, no narrative to sustain your writing. You're in the wispy world of parallels, metaphors, and other conceits. One forced phrase, one false step and your entire piece comes tumbling down in front of an audience that has been secretly hoping for just such a catastrophe.

Very, very few writers can bring this stunt off. Thoreau was a master at it. Several excellent nature writers can do it now and then. Fishing authors, in general, have racked up a miserable record, and, out of fairness to themselves and their readers, should keep their feet planted firmly on more familiar ground.

What, I'd like to know, is wrong with a lean, taut narrative, telling what a fishing incident was really like and making the reader feel he had been there? There are enough examples of this scattered through the pages of fishing literature to fill many bookshelves. Negley Farson's *Going Fishing* is packed with such writing from cover to cover, yet it seems to have escaped the attention of most self-appointed critics of fishing writing.

And what is wrong with a clear, crisp description of some tactic or technique that helps catch more fish? Does this, too, have to be embroidered with musings about the freckled cowslip, the jaunty jay or the majestic hemlock? Can't we enjoy our annual Maytime without moral uplift? There may be, as I've noted, a whole library of good paragraphs, pages, and even, occasionally, entire books on fishing, but there is also enough rot and rubbish by pretentious writers to fill fifty big stores devoted to remainders.

Two highly esteemed gentlemen come to mind here, and since both are dead there's little chance of hurting their feelings by citing them as examples. Henry Van Dyke and Bliss Perry were both ardent anglers and men of literary bent. Van Dyke, in particular, was widely acclaimed in his day and still has many admirers. Have you read any books by him lately? Or by Perry? I have, and I don't think I can stomach another fulsome phrase or mealymouthed moral for years to come. Both gentlemen would have you believe that fishing is an exercise in character development that would make the playing fields of Eton seem as self-indulgent as side-street stickball.

The spiritual descendants of these men and of Walton are with us today, of course. It wouldn't be fair to mention any names, for I have probably been guilty, myself, of the "Waltonian fallacy" no matter how hard I've fought to avoid it. Walton's influence is almost as strong and all-pervasive as original sin.

That just about winds up the case against Walton and, now that I've finished, a disturbing thought occurs to me: Perhaps I'm giving blame where blame isn't due. I may have been sniffing a cold trail while hounding the gentle Izaak. Perhaps he was a fine man, good friend, and great fisherman after all. Very possibly the real culprit lived many years earlier than the old plagiarist, whose only crime was pilfering an out-of-print book called *The Arte of Angling* — in which case the man I should be taking to task is that familiar and famous author, "Anon."

# 6

# Go Low and Slow for Big Salmon

Every month I see articles telling how to catch titanic trout, buster bronzebacks, colossal crappies, whopper walleyes, and the like. Yet I've never seen a piece on how to catch king-sized specimens of the king of fishes. Have you? Did you ever read anything about how to catch big Atlantic salmon?

Thirty years ago this topic might have been considered academic, for before World War II salmon were mainly the quarry of a privileged few. No longer. In 1973 an estimated 200,000 Americans (and nobody knows how many Canadians) fished for *Salmo salar*, and the numbers are increasing every year.

Despite its growing popularity, though, salmon fishing is rarely free, seldom cheap, often damnably expensive. Returning from a big-game, big-expense expedition like this with nothing over four or five pounds to show for your time, travel and camp fees can be disappointing, to say the least. Yet with salmon the rules are simpler and the odds more in your favor when angling selectively for big fish than in any other kind of freshwater fishing I know of.

By big salmon I don't necessarily mean thirty- to fifty-pounders. I know guides who have fished part of almost every day of the open season for years and have yet to land a salmon of this super-trophy size. But there are plenty of salmon in the ten- to twenty-five-pound class in every salmon river worthy of the name, and these are a whole different class of fish compared to the adolescent salmon of three to five pounds, called grilse, which make up the bulk of the catches on most popular rivers.

There are two reasons why most fish taken fall into this latter and less-than-heroic category. First, the more accessible rivers happen to have a high proportion of grilse in their run of fish. Why this is so, why a very few rivers contain mainly big fish while the others run to mostly small ones is hard to explain. One theory is that on some rivers the eight-inch young of the salmon, called smolts, which leave fresh water for the richer pastures of the ocean, may find their traditional feeding grounds nearby and tend to come back to their parent river in little more than a year, while fish from other river systems may travel so far that they don't return till after two or even three years of sea-feeding. Another theory suggests that, since all salmon return to the river of their birth for spawning, subspecies with different habits have been built up over the years. Whatever the reason, catches on some of the more popular rivers such as New Brunswick's Miramichi often run from three to five grilse for every mature salmon, while on others a fish of under ten pounds is a rarity.

The other reason the catch ratio often runs heavily to the grilse side is that grilse take a fly much more readily than older, larger salmon. This statement may baffle anglers who have heard that neither salmon nor grilse take food after their return to fresh water. The accepted explanation for this is that re-entry into fresh water awakens the insect-feeding reflexes these fish lived by during their early, trout-like life in the river. The longer the fish has been away at sea, this theory claims, the weaker this instinct will be when the fish returns.

Results in terms of catches certainly support this hypothesis. One year when the take on a New Brunswick river was running five grilse for every mature salmon, I went down to a bridge just above the head of tide to watch a run of fish moving up into the low, clear water. I was surprised to discover that the grilse/salmon ratio was about fifty-fifty. There were plenty of salmon coming into the river, including some very big ones, but they just weren't taking nearly as well as the grilse.

Similarly, there's a river in Newfoundland I have fished several times where camp records show that ten to twelve times as many grilse as salmon are caught year after year. I accepted this as a true sampling of the river population until one day when we lunched at the base of a falls that was impassable at that height of water. Here fish were piling up in large numbers and every few seconds a fish would make a futile leap for the lip above. From the sample we counted in over an hour, it appeared that here, too, the salmon were almost as numerous as the grilse, even though our ice house held ten times as many grilse.

Now don't jump to the conclusion that I am some sort of salmon snob. Grilse are marvelous fish. They would magnify and glorify any trout river in the world, bar none. They jump more often, put up a brighter, brisker fight than their more stately seniors, and often stage almost as long a fight. But, and this is a terribly important "but," salmon fishing brings out the big-game instinct in all of us. You don't go on safari in Africa to shoot 60-pound Thompson's gazelles. Nor do you invest all the time and money a good salmon trip takes to catch three- to five-pound grilse exclusively.

And, when it comes to grilse, that's about the size of it. There's an unwritten rule at most salmon camps that grilse are never weighed. They are "estimated" at five or six pounds by a tactful guide or camp operator, and this makes the angler happy. I have broken this gentleman's agreement on the sly often enough to know better. Having weighed and measured well over one hundred grilse from several rivers, I can cite the following figures with confidence: Grilse average twenty-two inches long and weigh a shade under four pounds. Some rivers in Britain have records of eleven-pound grilse (scale readings proved they had spent less than two years at sea) but the largest I have ever seen weighed five and a half pounds, while the smallest was a runt of eighteen inches and two pounds and a quarter. However, even these modest extremes are rare, in my experience. Nine grilse out of ten seem to fall within a fraction of the average.

At this point it would be encouraging if I could reveal the names of several undiscovered or neglected rivers where huge salmon pass upstream all day long unmolested by anglers. But I'm

afraid this can't be a fish-and-tell gambit. The few rivers where salmon average very large have been known, cherished, and bought up long before you and I were born.

For example, there are rivers in Norway where "ordinary" salmon will scale well over twenty pounds and where fish of over fifty pounds are killed each season. The rod fees there may run over $3,000 a week plus your transportation and other expenses. And, even if you have this kind of spending-money, you may have to stand in line for years to reserve a decent beat during a traditionally productive week in the short season.

In Canada, too, big-fish rivers like the Restigouche, Matapedia, Moise, and Grand Cascapedia have been mainly privately owned or controlled since before the turn of the century. On one of these rivers an acquaintance of mine once killed three salmon of over thirty-five pounds apiece in a single morning. However, the initiation fee to the club that controls this water, in case they invite you to join, is reported to be some $50,000 and dues $5,000 a year. After that you can pay for your two guides, food, accommodations, and tips with your leftover change. On the brighter side, though, if you're now feeling, as I am, like the kid with his nose pressed to the outside of the candy-store window, another acquaintance of mine once fished an equally rarified stretch of Canadian river for three full weeks and killed only two very mediocre fish!

If someone has been kind enough to leave you several miles of big-fish river complete with lodge or a vault full of blue-chip securities to buy your way in, read no further. You should catch plenty of big salmon without any advice from the cheap seats. If, on the other hand, you have to work for a living you can still catch some sizable salmon. Only in this case, more depends on *what* than *whom* you know.

The first thing you have to know is that most of the things you've learned about freshwater fishing don't hold true on a salmon river. Pay no attention, for example, to the old saying, "Big lure, big fish." It just doesn't work out that way in this type

*At Left:* Four mature salmon running from nine to twelve pounds. It would take at least ten grilse to weigh as much.

of fishing. A fly of one particular size will trigger the old, freshwater feeding instinct while, under the very same circumstances, one size smaller or larger may not. I have seen large salmon taken on a small #10 fly from the same pool where other anglers were simultaneously hooking only grilse with flies almost twice as large.

Admittedly, there is no exact rule regarding size of salmon fly, and this is one of the great mysteries — and charms — of salmon fishing. I have had to use flies two to three inches long (5/0s) to get the salmon's attention in the cold water of early spring in Spain. Even in the warm water of midsummer, you'll often have to use quite large flies to get results in the fifteen-foot or deeper pools on some very large rivers. However, it takes a big fly to interest the grilse, too, in this deep water and fly-size has apparently no influence on fish size.

A friend of mine who was new to salmon fishing once gave me a vivid example of this fact. We were fishing a very grilsey river in Labrador and my friend decided to concentrate on catching a truly big fish. He tied on a four-inch white bucktail he'd used for bluefish in salt water and fished it religiously all day. He took three grilse, by far the lowest score in camp. The rest of us had more fish and at least one good salmon apiece. Apparently, when there are that many fish in the river, you can find a few that will take anything, but most of them preferred the more modest #8s the rest of us were using.

Experienced trout fishermen will probably play a different hunch when trying to catch a trophy salmon. Since most big brown trout are caught at dusk or even after dark, they'll make their maximum effort after supper every evening.

The fact is, though, that salmon seldom take after dark. Perhaps the fly isn't visible enough in that weak light to activate the fish's nearly forgotten freshwater feeding instinct. Anyway, if there's even reasonable traveling water in a river, salmon will tend to continue their trip upriver at dusk and your chances of hitting a traveling fish on the nose with your fly are so slim that you might just as well forget night fishing altogether.

The trick of catching larger salmon is not, then, so much a matter of what you fish or when. It's *where* and *how* that will make the real difference. And of the two, *where* is perhaps the more important.

One of the least publicized facts about salmon is that they like, or will tolerate, slower water than grilse. Since these conditions usually occur farther downpool from the rapids at the head of it, salmon will usually be found in deeper water, too.

One famous pool on the Miramichi that I have fished for over twenty years is a textbook example of this. One side of this pool which is public water will host from fifteen to thirty fishermen all day long during the peak of the season. The fishing starts just below the shallow bar and by custom the anglers take a step down-current after each cast so that others can fish down the pool in turn. Some 150 yards downriver, where the current has slowed considerably, lies the traditional stepping-out point. This is marked by a jerry-built stone fireplace where fishermen warm up after their long immersion or boil a kettle of tea while waiting their turn at the head of the line.

The foreground angler is fishing the grilsey chop at the head of the pool. Distant angler is down into salmon water.

Over ninety percent of the fish I have seen taken in this conga line over the years have been grilse. The stretch is justly famous as one of the most productive on the entire river, but it produces very few salmon from either the public or the private side.

The price I willingly pay for fishing this choice water is the hour or more it takes me to work my way down-traffic to the fireplace. Below this, I have the rest of the pool—or "dead-water," as it is locally called—all to myself. Fortunately, this lower stretch lies around a slight bend and just out of sight of the anglers above.

I say "fortunately" because in the next two hundred yards I have caught more salmon and a higher percentage of salmon (including a twenty-pounder—my largest ever on the Miramichi) than on any other part of this river. The surprising thing is that, although I've told many friends about the productivity of the slow-water portion of this and other pools, I have had no company. I always seem to end up down there solo with a guide so disgusted that he soon goes to sleep. He does, that is, until I hook into a good salmon—which I do with pleasing regularity.

To go to the opposite extreme, which this same pool also illustrates, there's a small pocket just above the bar at the head of the pool. This slight indentation in the bottom can't be seen from the shore, yet it always seems to hold one and sometimes two grilse that have passed over the bar but not yet run the shallow rapids to the pool above. A guide I know often heads for this spot when the fishing gets slow and almost always hooks a fish there—much to the chagrin of the line of fishermen who have started in some hundred feet below. However, I have never, repeat *never*, seen a salmon hooked in that lie. It is apparently a grilse lie pure and simple—too fast and shallow to hold a big fish.

For some reason, guides—and they are mandatory for nonresident fishermen on salmon rivers throughout Canada—seem to favor grilsey water. This may be because the action is usually faster here and guides understandably like big tips from satisfied customers. However, and this surprises me, I find guides fishing these same grilsey lies on their days off when they're trying to pick up a fish for their own supper. Far be it from me to argue with a man who was born and raised on a river, but my advice to you is to fish a hundred or more yards down into the slower part of any pool—no matter how much your guide may grumble.

*How* you fish, even if you're casting over known big-salmon lies, can also affect the size of fish you take. Salmon are not only harder to rise to a fly, but they are also less likely to take a fly that is moving rapidly. I have seen many grilse rush at a fly that was whipping past them (and usually miss it), but I can't recall ever seeing a full-grown salmon behave in this manner.

The few times I have witnessed a salmon's rise to the fly from start to finish have borne out this theory. Salmon take as if they were in a trance (which seems to confirm the triggered-reflex theory) and without a trace of either greed or anger.

I was never more impressed by the robot-like quality of this rise than one noon when I was crossing a bridge to get back to my car. A guide was fishing by himself below me and I stopped to watch for a few moments since I had never seen an angler try this slow, deep water before.

When the unknown angler reached the bridge abutment below me, a salmon of ten to twelve pounds appeared below and behind his fly and then turned down and away again. I was so surprised by this sudden appearance that I said nothing, but put on my Polaroids to see if I could spot the salmon in his lie on the bottom. I couldn't make out the fish in that deep water, but then the angler, blocked from further downstream travel by the bridge, made another perfunctory cast from the same place. And this time I saw it all happen.

As the fly started to swing in toward the bank a shadowy form appeared about five feet away, rising slowly up through the water and quartering the current toward a point where it would surely intercept the fly. But again the fish stopped just short and drifted back down to his lie at exactly the same speed and on precisely the same course that he had taken on his exploratory trip toward the fly. The unhurried behavior and the precision of the course gave the impression that the salmon was some large, mechanical bathtub toy rather than a wild, living creature.

This time I yelled to the angler below who hadn't noticed me. I told him a salmon had come to his fly twice and he shot out another cast with renewed interest. Apparently, since the fish hadn't broken the surface either time, the fisherman had no idea he'd interested a good fish. I've since felt that this must happen to all of us more times than we imagine.

Even though the fisherman changed patterns twice, the results were the same: a near take or a last-minute refusal — whichever way you want to describe it. I thought the fly might be passing the fish's lie at too great a speed and suggested to the angler that he wade out deeper to try and get a slower swing over the fish. Out he went, but the deep water kept him right by the bank. I'm virtually certain that if he could have cast from ten feet farther out in the current, reduced the angle of his presentation and slowed down his fly, he would have taken that fish, but without a boat such a presentation was impossible.

The moral here is that, when in doubt, you should slow down the speed of travel of your wet fly. Many times I have heard salmon anglers claim that the best lies seem to be close to the bank they're fishing or that the most killing part of any presentation occurs during the last part of the swing when the fly is straightening out below them. I'm convinced, though, that the reason why so many fish are risen in the last moments of the presentation is that during the first part of it—the part that may well be covering the most productive big-fish lies — the fly is whipping over the fish at a speed too great to interest them at all.

To see why this is true, imagine a pool or run with a current speed that is the same from bank to bank. If you cast your line across this at the traditional 45-degree angle downstream with a perfectly straight line, you won't be fishing your fly effectively during the first half or more of your presentation. That portion of your line that enters the water nearest your rod-tip will, in a very few seconds, have traveled to a point directly downstream and will start playing crack-the-whip with your leader and fly which are still far across stream. The fly will only begin to fish properly when it is about ten degrees to one side of a straight downstream position.

The ways to defeat this disastrous effect are to cast downstream at a sharper angle when fishing fast water, mending the line near you in an upstream direction shortly after it enters the water or by casting an upstream curve in your line and then mending upstream as necessary. There's a nicety of judgment needed in

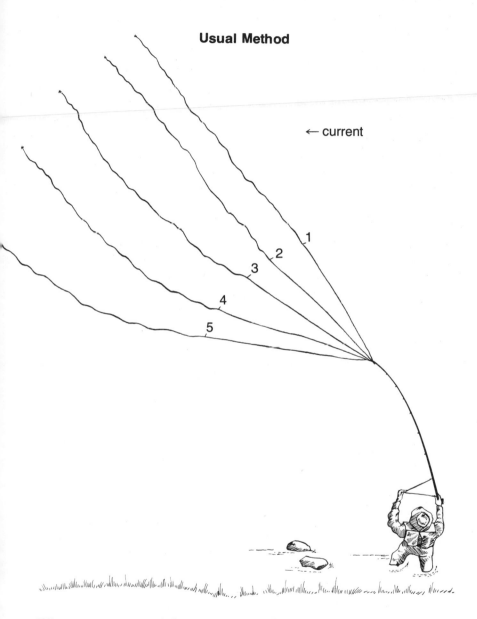

**Usual Method**

← current

1

2

3

4

5

When cast across and downstream the fly soon speeds up and fishes at proper speed only when just below angler's rod.

wet-fly presentations and, since the currents in every pool are different, there can be no pat answer. However, it is this ability to control the speed of travel of the fly that separates the expert from the chuck-and-chancer.

Presenting your fly *lower* in the water can sometimes be as important as fishing it *slower*. Big salmon are not only more reluctant to rise at all, but they are often less likely to rise all the way to the surface. I can't help wondering whether or not the angler by that bridge abutment wouldn't have taken that salmon if his fly had been riding a foot or so deeper in the current. After all, that would have reached the height from the river bottom to which that particular fish seemed willing to rise.

Fishing your fly deeper is axiomatic early in the morning or on raw days when the air is cooler than the water. Both salmon and grilse are notoriously shy about poking their noses out of a warmish river into cold air. When fishing your fly deep on a sinking line (weighted flies are forbidden by law) you may miss the thrill of seeing a classic head-and-tail rise to your fly, but that's not nearly as disappointing as no rise at all.

I have been presenting my fly lower and slower and casting it into deeper, slower water for twelve or fifteen years now. Every fish I hook isn't a huge salmon, but the *average* weight of fish I am now taking from grilsey rivers has nearly doubled with this change in tactics.

On one recent trip to the Miramichi when there was only a small run of fish my diary shows the following results. Our party of four took 27 fish that week and probably because I fished longer and harder than the others I accounted for nine of these. But seven of my nine were mature salmon while there were only two salmon in the other 18. As it turned out, my nine weighed slightly more than all the other fish put together.

The results of this and many other trips have been so rewarding that I recently described my theory and tactics to Charlie DeFeo. Charlie, I should explain, is one of the all-time great salmon-fly tyers and salmon fishermen. He has probably fished Canadian rivers for more days and over more years than any other living American. His opinions on salmon have nearly the weight of Supreme Court decisions.

## Correct Method

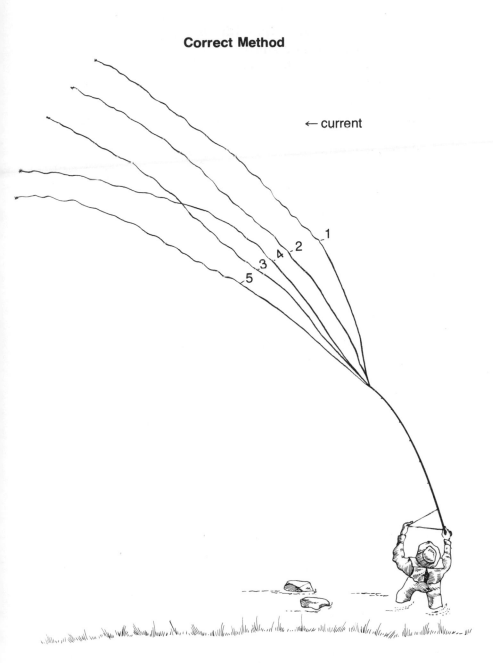

← current

By casting a curved line and then mending it upstream, as necessary, you can make fly travel at "taking" speed.

"The way you describe it," Charlie said, "reminds me of something Ira Gruber once said."

Ira Gruber, who died about ten years ago, may well have been the most expert and important salmon fisherman America has ever produced. He retired at an early age and devoted every summer until his death to fishing and understanding the Miramichi River. There he pioneered and developed many of the most popular flies used throughout Canada to this day. Over the years, he caught so many salmon that, once he'd hooked a fish properly, he's pass the rod over to his guide, pick up another one and continue his research on flies and presentations. Any man who managed to get that bored with playing salmon deserves to be a legend.

"I remember," Charlie continued, "back in the thirties Gruber once said to me that if half the fishermen made their flies swing slower and fished them down deeper there'd be darned few big salmon left in this river."

In times of scarcities like these, I'd hate to see that happen. I don't think it ever will with our new, lower bag limits. But, if lower and slower were the great Ira Gruber's secret formulas for catching big salmon, I know I've been on the right track for years.

# Long Live
# the Long Rod

I wish I had a day off to go fishing for every time I've heard a flyfisherman say something like ". . . they were mostly small fish, but since I was using that little six-foot rod of mine, I really had a ball."

My instantaneous reaction to such statements is, sure he did—if "ball" is short for balderdash.

For I'm convinced that the most overrated thing in America today (with the possible exception of home movies) is the short fly-rod. It is the least effective, least comfortable, least "sporting" fly-fishing tool ever invented for fishing running water. I know it's risky to knock another man's woman, dog, or favorite rod, but look at the evidence.

At first glance it may seen that the choice between a short rod and a long one for stream fishing is simply a matter of whim. After all, a fairly skilled caster can lay out sixty, seventy, or more feet of line with a tiny rod—more than enough distance for most trout-stream situations.

However, staying away from, and out of sight of, the fish is only a small, easy part of the game. It is the ability to present the right fly in a way that deceives the trout and the knack of hooking those you've fooled that separate the fishermen from the casters. And here, the short rod short-changes you in any number of ways.

A stubby rod leaves far too much line on the water while you're fishing out the average cast, and every extra foot of this is a crippling disadvantage, whether you're presenting a dry fly, wet fly, nymph, streamer, or (forgive me, Federation of Fly Fishers) live bait.

Suppose, for example, you're casting to a fish thirty feet away. With a six-foot rod, tip held high, you'll probably still leave eighteen feet of line and leader on the water when you make your presentation. A bit more when fishing upstream, a bit less when working downstream. On the other hand, with a ten-foot rod, casting under the same conditions, only about ten feet of terminal tackle—perhaps just your leader—would be lying on the surface. You judge which presentation is most likely to give you a badly dragging dry fly or a sunk fly that's traveling unnaturally and out of control.

Admittedly, the amount of line on the water isn't a critical factor when you're fishing a still-water pond or lake. But remember, my complaint about short rods was made about running-water fishing. And on streams with braiding currents, tongues of fast water, and unpredictable eddies, the more line you have on the water the more you're inviting an unappetizing presentation of your fly.

It is also much easier to hook a fish when most of your line is off the water. You're in more intimate touch with your fly and you don't have to guess at how hard to tug to straighten out the esses in your line, overcome the friction of water, and then set the hook delicately. Over ninety percent of the trout broken off are lost at the strike. Examine the circumstances the next time you leave your fly in a fish. I think you'll agree that the problem nearly always is too much line on the water when the take occurs.

It took me years to learn these simple fly-fishing facts of life. The truth started to sink in only about a dozen years ago when I was fishing in the mountains of southern France. I was using a snappy, eight-foot rod (certainly a sensible length by eastern U.S. standards), but I wasn't catching many fish and almost no really

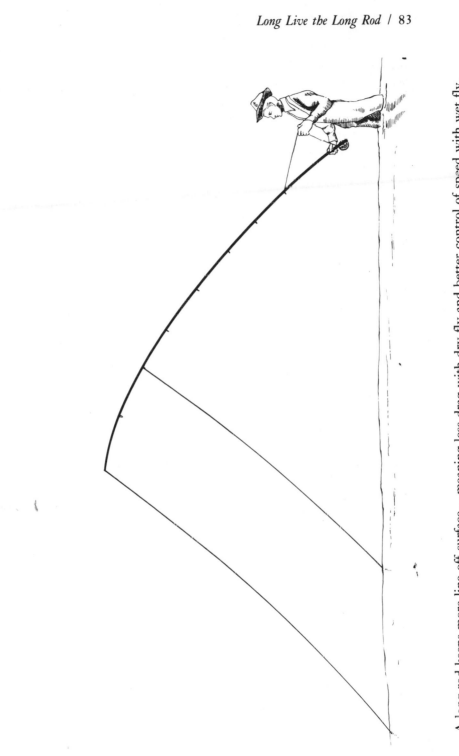

A long rod keeps more line off surface—meaning less drag with dry fly and better control of speed with wet fly.

good ones. This was slow, clear, limestone water, heavily fished by vacationers and constantly harvested by a troup of professional fishermen who supplied the local hotels. Any fish that had run this gauntlet and grown to decent size was as carefully trained as a moonshot astronaut.

The professionals finally showed me their secret—though they looked on it more as common sense than as an ingenious technique. They'd learned that, in this clear, slick water, they couldn't approach these fish from upstream. Yet neither could they give the trout a look at their leader. So they cast upstream to a rising or observed fish, but with a variation of the conventional method. They'd drop their fly—usually a sparsely dressed wet pattern on a light hook — just downstream of the trout's tail so the leader wouldn't pass over his head. When the tiny ripples from the fly's entry passed over the trout's nose, he would usually turn around to see what sort of insect had fallen into the water behind him. If the stunt was pulled off perfectly, all the trout could see now was the artificial sinking slowly down-current. No leader showed at all because it would be pointing directly away, behind the fly.

Any line splash or drag meant instant failure, and I began to see why these experts, who supported their families with their catches all summer, used long rods—ten to ten and one-half feet long, in fact. "With a rod of three meters you are just beginning to fish," they told me. Three meters — that's nine feet, ten inches. Their long rods let them cover a fish from a safe distance with only part of the leader entering the water. I finally learned how to execute this presentation with occasional success after days of practice, but my eight-foot rod, even though it could throw seventy to eighty feet of line with ease, was a big handicap here.

Fishermen I saw in the Pyrenees on the Spanish border had taken this theory one step further. They used rods twelve to fourteen feet long on the tumbling mountain streams and these kept so much line off the water that there wasn't even a word for "drag" in their local *patois*. They would simply swing their fly (or more often maggot) directly up-current and let it drift back naturally, keeping in touch by raising the rod-tip. They neither added nor took in line, but they took in trout with such regularity that a really devout conservationist wouldn't even mention this method.

   The implications of all this are enormous to the dry-fly man with his almost paranoid fear of drag. The perfect presentation of his fly has to be one dapped on the surface with no leader at all touching the water. This is as true whether the offering is to be made dead drift with the natural flow of the current or whether the fly is to be bounced on the surface like a hovering or egg-laying insect.

   I proved this to my satisfaction several years ago after a neighbor of mine had been given an ancient and enormous English fly rod. This awesome wand was a full twenty feet long, was made of a solid wood called greenheart, and must have weighed over three pounds. However, this 36-ounce beauty had a light, flexible tip—

A professional French fisherman with a twelve-foot rod fishing upstream without taking in or letting out line.

it was built when single strands of horsehair were used as leader-tippets—and I decided to try out a hunch with it.

I found some pretext to borrow this rod for a couple of hours and, after I'd rigged it up with a light line and fine leader, I headed for a nearby river. Once I got the hang of it, I could dap a fly on the surface thirty to 35 feet away and make it dance and hop there with no leader at all touching the water. Smart, overfished trout nearly herneated themselves to grab my fly. If I'd continued to use that rod the State Conservation Department would have named me Public Enemy No. 1. However, my friend soon retired the rod to his collector's case and perhaps that was just as well. After two hours with that wagon-tongue, I felt as if I'd slipped every disc in my back. I guess they don't build men the way they used to, either.

Until a hundred years ago most trout rods were twelve feet long. Two centuries before that they ran up to a healthy eighteen.

Going to the opposite extreme, you can cast and catch fish with no rod at all. This would give you a rod some twenty feet shorter than the old English muscle-builder I just described. I have never seen anyone over five years old fishing a trout stream with a handline, which would have to be the worst possible tackle for trouting. However, the reason is not that you couldn't cover the water or land the fish.

The late Ellis Newman could take the reel off the rod and with his bare right hand work out all ninety feet of a double-taper and keep it in the air, false-casting. Perhaps you could, too, if you practiced long enough. But would you catch as many trout that way?

Similarly, Lee Wulff once hand-cast to a nearby salmon and played that full-grown fish to the beach with just the reel in his hand. No rod at all. Again, you might do that, too, with practice. You might be able to dine out on this feat for weeks if you could tell the epic story with enough suspense and gusto. But I don't think you'd want to make a habit of fishing like that.

So you see, a fly-rod isn't a necessity. It's merely a convenience and a comfort.

How can I say "comfort" after that twenty-footer nearly put me in bed under traction? And doesn't a long rod have to punish the angler more than a short one? Well, yes and no.

In the first place, sheer lightness in a rod doesn't necessarily mean less effort. The difference between a five-ounce rod and a longer two-ounce model in ratio to the angler's total weight on the scales is about the same as drinking half a tumbler of water or going thirsty. So rest assured that the longer, slightly heavier rod won't weigh you down.

I have fished with many superb casters who said they revelled in the lightness of their short rods. But how they huffed and puffed and sweated. They were using both arms, both shoulders, and their back to make those long casts with their toy tackle. Double-hauling may be the ultimate technique for tournament casting, but it's about as placid a way to enjoy a summer evening as alligator wrestling.

The point is, ask not what you can do for the rod, but rather what the rod can do for you. With a long rod, a small movement of the arm or wrist will take any reasonable length of line off the water for the back-cast because there really isn't that much line clutched by surface tension. The line then goes back over your head, straightens out, and bends the rod backwards. Now a minimal effort forward with forearm, wrist, or both, and the rod snaps back, propelling the line forward again. What could be easier than that? The rod has done most of the work for you. Your hand has moved a foot or so with very little exertion instead of moving three feet or so and bringing shoulder and back muscles into play, as well.

My experiences in France were not the only reason my rods became longer about a dozen years ago. At approximately that time, I read an article in an outdoor magazine extolling the joys of minirod fishing. The author honestly admitted that he did, at first, have trouble avoiding drag with his shorter rod, but that he had solved this problem by holding the rod high above his head as he fished out every cast. Thus his six-footer, he claimed, was every bit as effective as an eight- or eight-and-a-half-footer and (get this) because his rod weighed only 1¾ ounces, it was far less fatiguing to fish with. Anyone who subscribes to that theory should now hold his right arm fully extended over his head for two or three minutes and tell me how it feels. I can't recall seeing any more articles from this man and I can only assume that acute bursitis has prevented him from taking pencil in hand ever since.

If a twenty-footer can break your back and a six-footer gives you too much drag and too much work, what length should an efficient and comfortable fly rod be? A lot depends on your physical makeup and your style of fishing. If, on the one hand, you're a continuous and compulsive false-caster who likes to fish pocket water upstream where the effective float is a foot or less, any rod over eight feet might put your arm in a sling. If, on the other hand, your style is more deliberate and you spend most of your time on slower water where you may make fewer than ten casts per minute instead of nearly a hundred, you could probably handle a ten-footer with ease for a whole day's fishing.

And don't be misled by the "bush-rod" addicts. They argue that you get hung up too often fishing small, overgrown streams if you use anything longer than a five-footer. But the fact is, you'll get hung up a lot with a very short rod, too, because any form of true casting here will put your fly and leader in the branches. A long line presentation is seldom an effective way to fish a string of small pot-holes, anyway. Drag is instantaneous and disastrous with a lot of line out on this type of water. Here, you're far better off with the long rod, flipping or swinging your fly to the chosen spot while you make the extra effort to conceal yourself.

Use as long a rod as you comfortably can. I have been fishing with an 8½-foot bamboo that weighs 4½ ounces for the past several years. I am now going through a trial-marriage with a 9½-foot glass rod that weighs about the same. This liaison has been so enjoyable that I'm now searching for a ten-footer with the same qualities.

On salmon rivers where I make only four or five casts per minute, my favorite wet-fly rod is a 10½-footer that works beautifully with a medium-weight #6 line. But I'll admit that I have to drop back to an 8½-foot stick for dry-fly fishing. I just can't false-cast that often with the long rod—although that

The author fishing across stream with a favorite 9½-footer. High rod-tip keeps even more line off water.

10½-footer is the most effortless wet-fly rod I've ever hefted. And let me repeat: I find all these rods, both trout and salmon models, comfortable for a full day's fishing.

In case you're interested, the man who wields these monster rods bears no resemblance to King Kong. I don't tip the scales at 140 pounds with chest waders, spare reels, and enough assorted fly boxes to drown me if I fell into deep water.

I'll have to admit, though, there's one disadvantage to long fly rods — and it's a beauty. When you've finally hooked a fish, the long rod makes the fish grow stronger. For that extra length gives the fish greater leverage against your hand.

But isn't this precisely what the short-rod people are espousing? That fish are now smaller and tamer so we must use tackle that magnifies the quarry? Yet aren't they actually doing just the opposite?

There are only two basic ways to measure a rod's ability to glorify the struggles of a fish. One is the weight or force it takes to bend the rod properly. This factor is usually printed on the rod just in front of the cork grip in terms of the weight of line it takes to bring out its action. I've seen a lot of 6-foot rods that call for a #6 or #7 line to make them work properly. This means that it takes between 160 and 185 grains (437½ grains equal one ounce) of moving line to flex the rod adequately. My 9½-footer, on the other hand, needs only a #4, or 120 grains, to flex the rod to its optimum. Draw your own conclusions.

But there's yet another factor that makes one rod more sporting than another for playing a fish. That's the leverage against your hand. With a fly rod—which must be considered a simple lever once a fish is hooked — the fulcrum is where the hand holds the rod. You don't need an M.I.T. degree to see that the mechanical advantage is approximately fifty percent greater in favor of the fish and against the sportsman with a nine-foot rod than it is with a six-footer.

Despite this elementary fact, I am often accused of derricking small fish out of the water with a whacking great salmon rod. Fault my reasoning if you can: I'm convinced the shoe is on the other foot. I maintain that short-rodders are not only selling themselves short on presentation and overexercising themselves needlessly, but grinding down small fish with mechanically superior weapons, as well.

If you have followed my argument carefully so far and, I hope, found it airtight, you're probably asking, "How can so many of nature's noblemen have been taken in by this cruel hoax?" The answer is a believe-it-or-notter that would have Ripley sitting on the edge of his chair.

In the beginning, all rods were long. They were used to swing some lure out to the unsuspecting fish and to haul the catch back to shore again. They were very much like our present-day cane poles and probably just about as long.

Rods were still very long in the seventeenth century. Izaak Walton recommends a snappy eighteen-foot, two-handed model as the best choice in his day. He and Charles Cotton dapped, dibbled, and dangled their flies (and worms and maggots) on the water with these mighty poles with killing effect on the trout — and probably on their backs, too.

A nine-foot rod gives the fish a fifty percent greater mechanical advantage *against* the angler than a six-footer does.

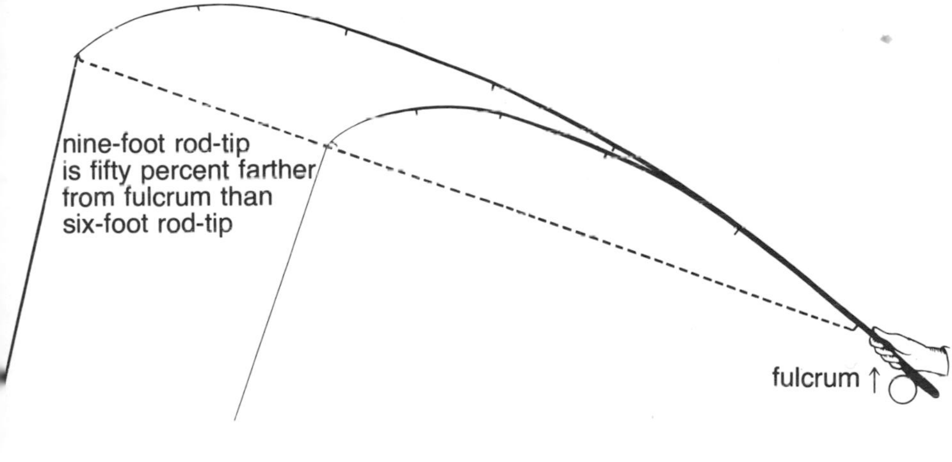

nine-foot rod-tip
is fifty percent farther
from fulcrum than
six-foot rod-tip

fulcrum ↑

In the following century the scientific progress of the industrial revolution reached the angling world. Fishing reels appeared on the market and soon became popular because they allowed fishermen to lengthen or shorten line easily and to play larger fish more effectively. But the rods themselves remained long.

One hundred years after that, in the not-too-distant 1800s, rods still averaged a sensible twelve feet until dressed silk fly lines and split bamboo were introduced just after the midpoint of the century. This made true fly-casting, as we now know it, possible for the average angler and, as this novel technique became popular, rods grew shorter and lighter. After all, why should the angler stand there waving half a tree over the water when he could cast to the far bank and beyond with a zippy little ten-footer?

But along with these advances came another type of progress: overpopulation, overfishing, and pollution. Trout became fewer and farther between. Fishing could no longer be the simple culling of nature's bounty as it had been in Walton's day. It needed a mystique, a philosophy, a *raison d'être*. This, Frederick M. Halford and other British Victorians readily provided, and their code soon spread across the Atlantic in a slightly modified form. If the sheer joy of catching fish was no longer a sure thing, at least there was the joy of casting. A day astream, the play of the sweet bamboo, the lovely hiss of the line, the fly cocked perkily on the sparkling riffle—who cares for a full creel with all this? You've read it all a hundred times in a hundred different forms. (I've even seen true believers act annoyed when an occasional hooked fish interrupted the rhythm of this ritual!) Under this type of credo, it's easy to see how rods were miniaturized into today's six-foot toys.

All the while, of course, anglers still secretly wanted to catch fish—and I suppose you do, too. But our artificial Victorian code insists that this be done only by improving your casting or presentation or by tinkering up a bit better imitation of, say, the female Iron Blue Dun. Reverting to aboriginal tackle and the more varied presentations it puts at your fingertips is unthinkable.

Well, I for one think it *is* thinkable. And, if you really want to catch more trout and enjoy more sport doing it, perhaps you should think about it, too. Going back to eighteen-foot poles might be a bit much. But do try a new nine or ten-footer. If a ribbon-clerk like me can swing one all day long, you'll be able to handle one like a conductor's baton.

Can't I, after all this, find at least one kind thing to say about our new short fly rods? Well, yes, perhaps this. I am reminded of the country sage's defense of bad breath. "It's mighty unpleasant, but it sure beats no breath at all."

So I guess short fly rods beat handlines—or no rods at all. But not by very much.

# The Backyard Angler

Every time I am introduced to somebody as "a fisherman" the conversation seems to start out like this.

"So you like fishing, eh? Then you probably know my friend Marmaduke—we call him Duke—Thornberry."

"Well, no. That name doesn't ring a bell. Does he fish around here often?"

"Oh no. Duke's a *real* fisherman. Spends two or three weeks every summer up near the Arctic Circle. You ought to see the fish *he* brings back. Yeah, Duke is some kind of fisherman, all right."

Sure he is, and it's not too hard to figure out what kind. Nine will get you ten that Duke is a very mediocre fisherman, indeed, if that's where he's done all his fishing.

For, wonderful as wilderness waters may be, as schools for fishermen they're about as useful as shooting galleries are for hunters. Hauling in unsophisticated fish, cast after cast, may build ego and even muscles, but it certainly doesn't build skill. In fact, I've found it can get so monotonous that I don't see how old Duke can stand it for three whole weeks unless he has several packs of cards and cases of whiskey along.

I'll admit the man is probably an accomplished caster by now and he should be able to play a fish in his sleep. But if he's done all his fishing in the true wilderness, chances are he doesn't know much about reading water, stalking fish, choice of flies or lures, and delicate presentation. And this is what fishing, as opposed to catching, is all about.

These facts were first impressed on me during a trip to a far northern salmon river which was undergoing a heavy run of sea trout. The first one I landed was a brightly colored male of about three pounds. I held him in my hands with proper reverence and returned him only after looking him over as long as I dared keep him out of water. At that time I could count on the fingers of one hand the number of wild brook trout that big I had caught in my entire life. But some fifteen trout later those beauties were becoming bores. They were grabbing the fly before the more stately salmon had a chance, and I was shaking them off as if they were chubs.

The last straw came a short time later while I was waiting for the guide to bring up the boat and take me to a less infested pool. I happened to peer into the eddy behind the rock I was standing on and saw a measly one-pounder loafing in the slack water. Out of boredom, I dropped the #6 double-hooked salmon fly in front of him. He was so close to my boots I had to hold the leader in my bare hand and dangle it down to him.

The trout had that big fly in an instant, but I yanked too hard and back came my fly with half the fish's upper lip attached to it. As I was removing this piece of gristle from the barb, I glanced down into the pocket below me again and saw the trout was still there. I knew it was the same one all right because the left half of his face was missing. On a hunch, I dropped the fly back down and—you guessed it—he savaged it instantly. This time he stayed on the hook and since I felt sorry for the maimed fish, I put him out of his misery and tucked him away for breakfast.

That handsome fourteen-inch brookie would have made the day on the Beaverkill or the Battenkill, but he was a tiddler up there. And his capture merely proved what I already knew from previous experiences. Wilderness fish are nothing at all like heavily fished trout: Their survival depends on getting to the food first in an extremely competitive situation while the reverse is true of trout living near centers of civilization. Only those that are wary and circumspect make it to maturity.

This is the reason why most of the great fishermen—the ones

who have made inventive and lasting contributions to our sport—have been the ones who fished close to home most of the time. Make your own list and check it out, but I think in the area of modern fly-fishing for trout any collection would have to list these names: Halford, Skues, Gordon, La Branche, Hewitt, Fox, and Marinaro.

Frederick M. Halford fished the chalkstreams of southern England for years perfecting and systematizing dry-fly practice and patterns. G.E.M. Skues invented the nymph and nymph fishing on the same waters. Theodore Gordon interpreted the dry fly into an original American art form and proved it out on our eastern rivers—but not until he had retired to the Catskills to fish the upper Beaverkill and Neversink exclusively for nearly twenty years. La Branche contributed his method of pounding up trout with the dry fly in fast water from his years of fishing a very few Catskill streams over and over again. Hewitt, perhaps the most original and inventive angler in history, designed the skater, pioneered the nymph on our waters, and invented countless other flies and improvements. Yet all his big innovations came *after* he had settled on the Neversink and fished it religiously every season. Fox and Marinaro gave us their jassids, midges, and terrestrials from their years of observation and experimentation on a very few Pennsylvania limestone streams.

Granted, all these men sometimes fished other areas. But their main contributions came from concentrating on their near-home fishing.

Granted, too, none of the advances cited are universally effective. Halford's theory of casting only to rising fish didn't work well on Gordon's rivers. La Branche's method of prospecting fast water isn't much use on Fox's and Marinaro's placid limestone streams, nor are the latters' meadow-born jassids, in turn, much use in the forests of the Catskills. But all these techniques work often enough and in enough places to be invaluable additions to the trout fisherman's arsenal.

This, by the way, is meant in no way to belittle the many excellent books by expert anglers that have taught people how to cast, identify flies, tie artificials, and learn streamcraft. Many of these have been beautifully written, are extremely useful, and are classics in their own right. But it is a singular fact that the men who have brought us the major forward leaps are remembered as the truly great ones and all have been basically stay-at-homes.

The reason for this, I think, is that one man can do only so much in his fishing lifetime. Apparently it takes many years of painstaking observation before the intuitive leap to discovery takes place, and then many more years of trial and error to refine the idea into a usable practice. When there are too many variables in place, conditions, and happenings this flash of understanding rarely occurs.

Then, too, the man fishing exotic, remote places is seldom really challenged. If one fish proves stubborn, there are many more willing — and perhaps bigger — ones waiting for the next cast. Truly rotten fishing is tedious, of course. But demanding fishing makes the great anglers. Gordon was one of the first writers to emphasize this point. Over and over again in his letters he told how he turned down offers of easy fishing on heavily stocked waters because he learned nothing there and found it uninteresting.

Classic wet and dry flies sit harmoniously side by side on a fly-tyer's table. This could never happen in Halford's day!

G.E.M. Skues may look stodgy and proper enough to us, but he was an anti-establishment free-thinker to Edwardians.

When you're continually fishing new and different waters — even if they're not overstocked and too easy — the chances are against your learning anything new and important from them. Here you're usually under the care of a sponsoring host or an expert guide—either of whom knows the lies and the habits of the fish so well that you're spared the enlightening agony of finding out what it has taken them several years of trial and error to discover. Only the most introspective and analytical angler begins to question and research when he is placed in the prime places at the best time with a taking fly and is catching fish at a satisfactory rate.

This is one of the few things I find displeasing about Atlantic salmon fishing. You are usually accompanied by a guide, and in Canada you must be by law. This local expert takes you to a pool, tells you what fly to put on, where to start in, and how to angle your cast. If you're on new water, this service can be invaluable. But do you need—or want—this day after day? Once you've been shown the most likely holding spots, it's a lot more fun (and often more productive) to experiment with other types of flies and techniques. For example, I caught all my salmon last September on the dry fly though I fished it only ten percent of the time because the guide had told me it just wouldn't work at that time of year.

The art of reeling in a fish — no matter how hard it may struggle — is the least absorbing part of the game. Men I know who specialize in tarpon, bonefish, or salmon always tell me that what attracts them is the peerless fighting quality of the quarry, but I don't completely believe them. That may be part of the excitement, but their main involvement lies in making the fish strike under all—especially difficult—conditions. The subsequent battle is merely the frosting on the cake.

No, the reeling in and netting of a fish may be the finale of any fishing episode, but it's certainly not the climax. It's when you've induced the fish to hit and felt you've hooked him solidly that the main satisfaction occurs. People who merely harvest fish— something most of us only dream about—seldom enjoy fishing. I knew many New England coastal fishermen in my youth who spent all day under treacherous conditions hauling in nets and trot lines from the sea. Not a one of them would go fishing with me with rod and line. They seemed to think that taking a few fish, the hard way, on rod and reel was merely a busman's holiday.

Similarly, the best salmon guide I have ever met couldn't understand why we "sports" from America would put in the long hours under awful conditions to take fish which we usually released. He was caretaker of a small camp on a desolate northern river, and he knew every lie as well as a tongue knows a sore tooth. I saw him fish for himself a few times and it was a sobering experience. He would step out on a rock in front of camp, cast expertly to a known lie, hook, land his fish, and be back to his cabin in fifteen minutes. But you could see that it was just another daily duty to him like splitting kindling, lugging in spring water, or opening a can of beans. He was in no way interested or challenged. Since even some of the more persistent visitors to this river could hook up to fifty salmon and grilse a day during the times when the salmon were running well, the whole drill was a bore and a chore to him.

Of course, everyone wants to fish new and better waters from time to time for a change of pace or scene, even if he doesn't have a pet theory to try out under other conditions. And everyone deserves the exhilaration of catching too many fish once in a while after the usual weeks or months of catching too few. But enough is enough, and sometimes overkill is worse than underkill. I remember once fishing for bonefish with a very young and inexperienced angler when the water was too cold and the fish few and choosey. After two days with one fish between us I decided he might quit fishing forever if things didn't pick up. That afternoon we hired a guide who took us to a small channel hole that was paved with bottom fish. We took fish on nearly every cast—mostly grunts, porgies, yellowtails, and triggerfish that fought very well for their size—until we had a glass-bottomed bucket filled with these panfish. After about an hour my young companion either got his belly full or got the idea. He turned to me and said, "The tide seems to be coming in again now. Do you think there might be a few bonefish up on the flats?"

For every fisherman who thinks difficult fishing is bad fishing there seems to be two who think that their nearby waters are poor simply because they are nearby. Familiarity can breed too much contempt. I know a fisherman who averages several trout each fishing day that run from one to three-and-a-half pounds. Remember, that's his *average*. On good days he often takes ten or more such fish. All are taken on the dry fly from a public river that's within a three-hour drive of New York City. His secret? He lives nearby, fishes almost every day of the open season, and has done so for years. He knows the lies, the flies, which stretches produce best at different times of day and under different conditions and, perhaps most important of all, how to duck the crowds. It sounds incredible, but I've fished with the man and he really does that well.

So don't eat your heart out when you're doing your armchair fishing next winter and reading tales of monster fish being piled up like cordwood. Fishing on your own familiar, home waters can be not only productive—it can be even more rewarding than some safari to the land of the Leviathans. All that's gold does not necessarily glitter.

Think of it this way: Aren't you always more comfortable and content in your familiar bed in your own home than you are in someone's guest room or in a hotel? No matter how luxurious your strange new quarters may be? Almost everyone is.

A stream, river, or lake is like that, too. It's not just that you may be familiar with the shoals and hazards of a stillwater or the slippery ledge-rocks and deceptive drop-offs in a river. You also know approximately how many fish, and what sizes, to expect from past experiences or observations, and you can concentrate on catching some of them. On unfamiliar waters, however, if you don't see or take a fish in the first hour or so you can easily become convinced the place is fishless and thus lose heart.

Most important of all, memories of past occurrences — of fish caught or merely seen — in that exact place add excitement and anticipation to every cast. Few of us fish to revive old memories, but they do come back whether we wish it or not when we revisit familiar territory and they add richness to the day. Hemingway's famous story, "Big Two-Hearted River," shows he felt this way, too.

The best day's bass fishing I ever experienced was far from the most enjoyable one. A friend and I had portaged a canoe into a

102 / FLY-FISHING HERESIES

small Canadian lake that hadn't been fished in years. We caught only a few small fish during the first two hours and were thinking of turning back when we hit the jackpot.

We had pulled the canoe up onto an undercut rock ledge to eat lunch when I spotted a bass drifting out from under this hidden lie. I called to my companion and quickly we both started casting. His aim was better than mine and he hooked the fish, but I wasn't disappointed for long. A huge school of smallmouths poured out into the open, fighting to get the minnows the hooked fish was choking up as he fought.

I've never seen anything like it before or since. One of us played a hooked fish to keep the school nearby while the other picked out a postgraduate and cast to it. If a freshman of under two pounds came near the fly the cast was made again. I kept count of the fish landed — not just hooked — for a while, but gave up after we passed seventy-five. We must have caught and released nearly fifty smallmouths apiece — each more than 2½ pounds — in less than two hours. We kept two of over five pounds and then called it a day even though the bass were still hitting on every cast.

A few weeks later that same season I made a weekend visit to the lake in central New England where I had spent all my childhood summers. During those carefree years I had canoed, fished, lived on that lake from sun-up to dark, and I knew every inch of shoreline, every sunken boulder, ledge, or drop-off as I will never know any other body of water no matter how long I live. Even during my childhood there had been too many motor-boats, too many fishermen, and not too many fish here. The man who ran the boat livery said it had been getting even worse for several years. How right he was.

I worked like a bird dog all day long finding every favorite spot and using every secret stratagem I'd worked out as a boy, and I didn't give up till dark. My twelve hours' rowing and casting had netted me two bass well below bragging size — one just over a pound and the other not quite two. I'll admit I was pleased with the expression on the boat-renter's face when I held up what were apparently the first two bass brought back that week, but that was far from the best part of the day.

I hadn't fished that lake for over a decade, yet I had been able to locate every special fishing place unerringly. Each underwater rock, ledge, shoal, or weedbed was just where I'd left it and hadn't withered or wrinkled a bit with age. When I made a cast after a cautious approach, big fish seen or caught here years before seemed to be following my fly or rising up under my bass-bug. That day was a full program of instant-replays, and I was so absorbed that the great bass bonanza that I'd lucked into a few weeks earlier never crossed my mind.

I'm quite sure I didn't draw any morals or precepts from that day's mediocre fishing at the time, but it appears that as an older dog now I still haven't learned any newer tricks. For the past fourteen years I have trout-fished on my home river for fifty to sixty days each season. On those few days when I wrench myself away to fish what may be a far more productive river I feel a keen sense of loss.

Late last July I went up salmon fishing in Canada to try out some experimental flies I had great hopes for. Admittedly this is the period of summer doldrums on Catskill rivers, but I felt I would be missing something important. There is a late-evening hatch of two small mayflies and one caddis at that time of year, and I had yet to work out a decent imitation of any of them. I came back from an interesting and fairly productive trip with a nagging sense of guilt. I knew that while I'd been indulging myself in salmon I'd lost a full year as far as solving a difficult but intriguing trout-fishing problem was concerned.

Though I may be a slave to this river, it is *voluntary* servitude and I wouldn't have it any other way. I watch the big fish spawn in November. I check the shallow eddies along the shoreline to get an idea of how early and how many eggs have hatched out in March and April. I read scale samples during the open season to determine growth rates. I study stomach contents. I tag fish to learn more about their seasonal movements. I put on mask and snorkel on warm days to try to understand why some lies hold several good fish while others, that seem as good to me, hold none. And I give the river a thorough physical after each flood or high water to see why pools, pockets, and cut-banks change the way they do and to predict where the best lies will occur next season.

Then there are all the insects to observe and imitate. Which species do the trout like best and which do they take half-heartedly? Is it possible to tell from the rise-form which insect is being taken? Which types are decimated by higher than usual spring floods and which are so hardy they contribute full hatches in bad years as well as in good? I spend as much of my time digging into questions like these as I do in testing my observations and theories in the delightful act of fishing.

Because of this I may now fish less than I used to, but I feel that I'm learning something and I enjoy each fishing hour that much more. Several mystery stories are unfolding simultaneously and the one titled, *Will I or won't I hook that eighteen-inch brown that lives under the willow root tonight?* is not always the most absorbing one.

I don't consider myself a fish-farmer in any sense of the word, and yet this familiar portion of the river is in many ways like a garden to me. Its seasonal changes and the progress of its crop of trout have the same fascination for me that the growth of a flower bed or vegetable plot does for the enthusiastic gardener.

And, as any gardener can tell you, no one else's garden is half as interesting as your own — no matter how lush or weed-free theirs may be. The French poet-philosopher Voltaire summed it up perfectly when he gave his famous formula for happiness: "Cultivate your own garden."

Some may interpret this as a sly hint to worm-fishers as to the best place for digging bait. However, I like to think it was the best and soundest advice ever given to us flyfishers, too.

# Spare the Rod and Spoil the Trip

Hundreds of thousands of American fishermen probably visit Europe each year but never think of bringing their rods and reels. More than forty million Americans cast a fly, hurl a plug, or dunk a worm at home each summer, yet I can't recall ever meeting another American fishing on the mainland of Europe. Perhaps the reason American anglers don't think of Europe (with the exception of the British Isles and maybe bits of Scandinavia) as fishing country is that it seems too civilized. This continent is known as museum-touring, cathedral-watching territory, and since there aren't any swarms of black flies, grunting Indians, or camp-raiding black bears, how can there be any fish?

Well, don't let the fact that your wife may be with you or that you're bathing and shaving regularly make you feel that fishing is gauche. You can find superb trout fishing without tears and tribulations here, and the fact that you dress and smell a little better, as you probably will on a continental tour, won't bother the trout a bit. By all means take some tackle with you next time you sacrifice some vacation to take your wife to Europe. And keep your eyes and ears open. You just might have the fishing trip of your life.

The surprising truth is that continental fishing runs from good to superb, despite the density of the human population. For centuries, good fisheries have been cherished and preserved—not democratically, perhaps, but preserved. Nearly all the productive lakes and streams are either privately owned or controlled by the State or an association. And yet, you can gain access to most of these waters by simply asking the right questions or by paying a modest fee.

When I first wangled several months' vacation and decided to fish my way through Europe, I had become accustomed to impersonal treatment in the great cities. I wasn't prepared for the reception I got from rural residents of the same countries. For example, I found Frenchman after Frenchman listening to me with courtesy, even with empathy, as I talked about fishing. The only explanation I can give for this is that there's a freemasonry among fishermen. When I appear with a rod instead of a *Guide Michelin* in my hands, I am treated as a fellow fisherman and not as "the American tourist."

A striking example of this hands-across-the-river understanding occurred early one trip while I was fishing the salmon rivers of

Casting my way down a salmon pool on the heroic Rio Narcea in Austrias, Spain, on a bluebird April afternoon.

northern Spain. My wife and I had put up at a small *fonda* upriver, near the fishing spots. The other guests were Europeans of a type we hadn't met on previous trips and haven't met since without persuasive letters of introduction. They were a young Spanish marquis, his cousin, son of some duke, and a chateau-owning Frenchman.

We soon found ourselves chatting together about the day's fishing, since all meals at this simple inn were set at a communal table. After dinner, the talk became more intimate and the marquis, quite suddenly, insisted on boosting me to an honorary peerage.

"Oh, I know there are no titles in America," he said, with the authority of a young man who had spent a year at an American college. "Things are very democratic. But, after all, a man who fishes for salmon . . ." He shrugged his shoulders and I began to sense the great cachet Europeans attach to salmon fishing. I was toying with the idea of accepting only a temporary knighthood— just to avoid an argument, mind you — when my wife, a devout commoner, vetoed the idea. The next evening these aristocrats explained in detail how they avoided paying income taxes—for a European, an intimate act of disclosure that rivals the sharing of a toothbrush.

I cannot promise that fishing is a surefire method for social climbing. Most of our fishing encounters have been far less lofty —though not necessarily less rewarding.

Trout fishing in Austria won't make you feel like a member of the nobility, but it will make you feel like a minor celebrity at times. Townspeople walking back from the day's haying wave and call out "Petri Heil," thus summoning for you the support of the fisherman's saint. And I remember supper, back at the fishing inn, with its ritual serving of the trout — which had been kept alive in a springhouse across the courtyard. Austrians would no more eat an hour-dead trout than a Down-Easter would cook a dead lobster. And the foreign fisherman quickly adjusts to the idea of keeping his catch alive for the springhouse. A waitress once asked how I would like my trout prepared and then dashed out with a huge brass key to unlock the springhouse and deliver the fish, still wriggling, into the hands of the cook. There is a

Live trout being poured from the barrel-like *Lagl* into a spring-water *Kälterer*. Austrians insist on fresh-killed trout.

reverence for trout in this countryside, and just a touch of it is also bestowed on the captor.

Our stay in the Cévennes Mountains of south-central France was the most enjoyable of all. People went out of their way to point out the choicest holding water, even the lies of legendary monsters. A few of our neighbors here were professional market fishermen who supported their families all summer with the trout they caught from these hard-fished public waters; yet, after a proper interval, they shared with me some of their secret fishing methods. One of these was especially ingenious.

Once the sun hit these clear waters, the sensible fish would tuck themselves under the overhanging willows near the banks. If you then approached them from upstream, or the direction they faced, they would spot you and sink out of sight before you could get within casting range. A midstream attack was out of the question because the channel was too deep for wading. And, when you tried to cast your dry fly above their noses from below, your line or leader fell to the water over their heads and they scattered in terror. These were frequently harassed, sophisticated fish. The solution the native fishermen offered was to deliver a small wet fly with a distinct "plop" to a point just behind the fish's tail. This slight noise and the spreading ripples caused by the entry would tease the trout into turning around to investigate, hoping an ant or beetle had fallen out of the foliage. The rest was a foregone conclusion.

One of the joys of our visit here was watching the children go after tiny fish called gudgeon. The kids cut their own rods on the spot every day—slim two-foot pieces of peeled willow. To such a rod they knotted a similar length of light monofilament, and at the extreme end of the line a small split shot, a miniature hook, and bait.

Their strategy was to lie down on a cutbank or large rock with just the head and right arm sticking over the edge. From this vantage point, the kids could see several of the small fish lying inert and almost perfectly camouflaged on the sand and pebbles. They then lowered their baited hook to the bottom, inched it up

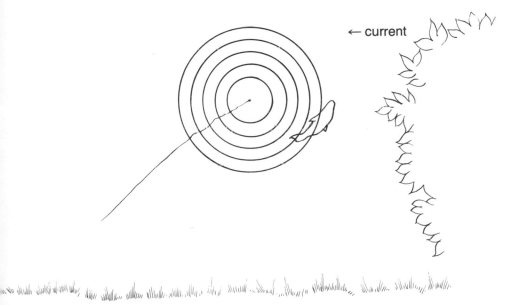

← current

Casting the wet fly behind the trout in the French manner. Gallic anglers know better than to cast above these fish.

to a fish's chin and, when it finally opened its mouth and took the bait, jerked this tiny fish up onto the bank.

Caught up in the enthusiasm of the mini-fishing, we gave it a go. It was certainly a far cry from past heroics on the salmon rivers. And yet, one had to exercise great skill and patience. There was a hidden reward to this child's play. The four-inch, dark-meated gudgeons turned out to be the only freshwater fish I've ever eaten that were even tastier than pink-fleshed, wild trout.

The finest trout fishing I have ever enjoyed anywhere, any-time, was on the Traun River in Austria, just below Gmunden at Marienbrucke. This choice water was controlled by the State, yet the license fee then was only two to three dollars a day. To give you an idea of the quality of this fishery, all trout under sixteen inches had to be returned according to the regulations. It was fly-fishing only—no bait, no spinning—yet most of the fish which rose were well over the minimum.

Unfortunately, the lower Traun has since been ruined by the erection of a dam, but there are other rivers in Austria and Yugoslavia that could rival this fishery. I have also enjoyed excellent trout fishing in Luxembourgh, Germany, and even in the crowded regions of France.

Don't be put off by those stories of $3,000-a-week rod fees on the famous rivers of Scotland and Norway—even though out-landish fees are charged in some areas. Some of the most productive fishing I ever had on the Continent was absolutely free simply because I was staying at the inn that controlled the water. I have never been charged as much a $5 a day for trout fishing. Two dollars per rod-day might be a fair average. I'll admit, though, that my salmon fishing in Spain was almost the price of an all-day lift ticket at an expensive ski resort. Accommodations, on the other hand, were so much cheaper that my two-week stay cost a good deal less than a fortnight's skiing in the Rockies.

How will a wife feel about a trip like this? I wouldn't try to tell you how to sell this bill of goods, but the facts are in your favor. Continental fishing is a far cry from the black-fly-and-bear-infested barrens of northern Canada. You are rarely more than a half-hour's drive from an excellent restaurant or interesting his-toric site. If the weather's rotten or the river is muddy, you can always go on an enjoyable day's excursion. When we were rained out in southern France, we'd spend the day in the cathedral town of Albi or at the Roquefort Caves, both of which were within an easy hour's drive. In Spain we'd visit the Altamira Caves or explore the picturesque coves and fishing towns of the north coast. At Gmunden, we'd drive into Salzburg, barely an hour away.

Even on perfect days, nobody flogs the water all day long. Dawn patrols are unheard of. Breakfast is leisurely and fishing usually starts at about ten. Afternoons are spent hiking, napping, birding, reading or doing whatever you like. You take the cream of the sport — a few hours in the morning and the best of the evening — and that's usually enough to satisfy anyone.

Nearly half the Europeans I met on these waters were accompanied by their wives. Very few of the women ever fished, but most had been going on these trips with their husbands for years and they seemed to enjoy their holiday as much as the men did.

Food and accommodations at European fishing inns are up to

An Austrian lady angler properly equipped with knee boots, wool skirt, and a sensible ten-foot fly rod.

the best the region affords and that is usually very good indeed. Life is, admittedly, a bit simpler than at the large Continental resort hotels. You won't find roulette, dancing or floor shows. On the other hand, there are no all-night, whiskey-drinking poker games, either.

Even the most primitive regions can come up with some surprising amenities. At that small *fonda* in northern Spain, I was assigned a *ganchero*, or guide, called "Chamberlain" — a name he had earned because he always carried an umbrella to protect his fisherman in case of rain.

Despite the single-minded purpose of my fishing trip, I was never very far from the world of art and architecture. One evening on a river in southern France, for example, I took a shortcut home through the woods and stumbled onto a superb, thirteenth-century chapel. I was surprised when I couldn't find any mention of it in the guidebooks covering the region. Later, the townspeople, who took its presence for granted, told me it was the only building left in the valley where their town used to be. More than 600 years ago everyone had moved up onto the cone-shaped hill nearby for protection during a long, and now almost forgotten, war.

Unlikely as it seems, my wife and I may be the only Americans who have ever seen that small church. Come to think of it, if I'd been off looking at cathedrals instead of fishing, I never would have found it at all.

Idyllic surroundings on the Mur in Austria. Dramatic scenery, quaint buildings, and no other fishermen.

# 10

# The World's Best
# Trout Fishing

When you daydream about trout fishing in the perfect place, where do you find yourself? In the Canadian subarctic with its big, beautiful brookies? At Lake Taupo, New Zealand, with its huge rainbows? Southern Chile with its oversized browns? The stately chalkstreams of England with their legendary, free-rising trout?

All of these places rate high on my list, but none reaches the very top. The brook trout of northern Canada are either impossible or too easy to catch, and I really don't enjoy playing blood-bank to clouds of black flies. Taupo rainbows are big and lively, but lakes have always been my second-choice location for trout fishing. Trout down near the tip of South America may average bigger than anywhere else in the world, and it's thrilling fishing if driving a large streamer into gale winds is your favorite exercise. And the water-meadows of Hampshire, for all their beauty and history, offer fishing that's a bit too picky for my taste, and besides, most of the fish you catch there today have been stocked.

No, I'd take Austria's River Traun, the stretch just below Gmunden, that I fished for part of two seasons fifteen years ago, over any other trout fishing I've seen or even heard about. Here was a pleasant, nearly bug-free climate, the most perfect fishing inn I've ever seen, the widest variety of fishing conditions on a single river, sport difficult enough to leave you with a sense of accomplishment yet not so demanding as to be frustrating, and a marvelous head of fish—including some enormous ones if trophy-hunting was on your agenda.

Don't pack your rods and waders, though. The Traun fishery was ruined about six years ago and all that's left is the memory. But it was good enough for a lifetime of those in the good old days.

Why reminisce about what no longer exists? Not simply for the taste of nostalgia, though there is that, admittedly. In part, I want to write about its delights for the same reason authors write about so many departed joys—to share them. But there is a more important motive, for I think there are lessons to be learned from the Traun. I would like American anglers to know just how good a river can be, and I would like them to know that it is not beyond possibility for us to establish and maintain our own Traun somewhere, someday. I indulge the hope that the question is not whether it can be done but how it can be done.

The first time I ever heard of this river was while talking fishing with an English diplomat at a party in Germany. After swapping several fish stories, he told me he thought the Traun at Marienbrucke offered the finest fishing on the Continent, very probably the best in all Europe. Somehow his description rang true and I jotted down the details for future reference. A few months later, when I had some spare time, I drove down through Austria to Gmunden with a trunkful of tackle and gear. I found the Marienbrucke Inn easily from his directions, parked my car, and prepared to enjoy a week's superb trout fishing.

Life was not to be that simple, though—not in Austria during the high season. I was told politely but firmly that the inn was full. When would they have a vacancy? Perhaps not for the rest of the summer. Most of their customers, I was told, were regulars who booked almost a year in advance. No wonder the fishing was excellent, I thought. You couldn't even get near it.

I was shaken, but couldn't believe things were as impossible as all that. I would spend the day sightseeing in the area, I said, and would return later in the day to see if something had opened up. I even went so far as to mention the diplomat's name to show I had some sort of credentials. There was a look of honest pity on the good innkeeper's face, and as I drove away I was not nearly as confident as my manner had indicated.

After a lovely lunch at the head of the Traun-see, the lake that stretched above Gmunden, I spent the afternoon gawking at the scenery of the Salzkammergut — grandeur that was temporarily wasted on a fidgety fisherman — and drove back to Marienbrucke trying to convince myself that something good was about to happen. The innkeeper's wife met me before I reached the door. I was incredibly lucky, she told me. They had just that minute received a cancellation by phone. A serious illness. She would send a boy out to my car to help me in with my gear.

I thought they were simply playing hard to get and congratulated myself on going along with their ploy. I was mistaken, however, as I soon learned by talking with other guests. You did, indeed, need to book far in advance and I had just won a thousand-to-one long shot.

The inn was perfect, and many North American fishing camps have much to learn from the comforts it provided: a room with racks for rods, nets, etc., and just inside that, a warming room for wet waders and outside gear. These first two rooms inside the door were for fishermen and fishing gear; after that, gracious living took over. Most bedrooms had a small balcony, comfortable beds, and pleasing decorations. Meals were excellent, sometimes even superb, offering a reasonable choice of home-cooked dishes

The beautiful Marienbrucke Inn viewed from across the still-water where monsters smash your tackle at dusk.

that were planned around a fisherman's hours, rather than vice versa. Breakfast was particularly large and enjoyable, and there was no noticeable rush for choice water. A 9:30 start was early enough even in midsummer, and desperate dawn patrols were unheard of. With these amenities you could convince even your wife that fishing and fishing camps can, indeed, be couth.

The fishing itself was usually so good you didn't have to overdo it, and there was an almost infinite variety of fish and fishing in the ten miles of water this fishery controlled. The size limits, which were strictly adhered to, give you some idea of the quality of this water. Grayling, which were considered only a cut above trash fish, could be taken at twelve inches. Brown trout had to be sixteen inches. And *Lachsforelle* (which translates into salmon-trout) had to be twenty inches. Such limits may seem like the rules set for "one-trophy-fish-only" stretches of some Eastern U.S. rivers, but the surprising fact was that on the Traun some eighty to ninety percent of the fish you took—even on the dry fly—were over these lofty limits. The fish themselves were in beautiful condition and absolutely wild. There was no record of the river ever having been stocked. A very few coarse fish shared this river with the trout: some *Ettel* (a large European chub) and a few *Hecht*, or pike. The chub seemed to serve no purpose and were few in number, but the occasional large pike probably kept the trout on their toes, weeded out weaklings, and thinned the younger generation so that the survivors had more to eat.

This portion of the Traun was the outflow of a ten-mile-long, glacial-groove lake and, unlike most lake-fed trout fisheries in the U.S., the water entering the lower part of the river came off the top of the lake rather than from some deep, cold subsurface pipe. Apparently, the lake was cool enough, due to glacial melting into feeder streams from the high surrounding mountains, so that the plankton-rich surface water was below the upper limit which trout will tolerate. If you've ever seen the breathtaking Salzkammergut, either in person or in pictures, you'll see why this may be a nearly unique situation.

Both the insect hatches and the trout were far larger than they were in the only slightly smaller inflow river ten miles up the lake. Were the windfall insects and the surface plankton responsible for this increase in fertility or did the treated sewage effluent from the small city of Gmunden (which straddled the outlet from the lake to the river) play its part, too? I never ran a test on a water sample to find out, but one thing or another certainly agreed with the lower Traun trout.

The water below Gmunden was more like a salmon river than a trout stream in size. It averaged only one hundred to one hundred and fifty feet wide, but the banks were so firm in most places that it had dug itself down into the deep, big-rocked layer of its bed. I never found a place I could cross it — even in August dead-low water — with chest waders. The river had variety to surpass its size; every mile contained a full choice of every type of trout habitat imaginable. There were long, deep still-waters, dams, plunge-pools, runs, rapids, classic pools, pocket-water, and flats repeated again and again with foot or car bridges every mile or so to let you cross over.

If I could have one more day on this water, as it once was, I would fish it as I never did when it seemed sure to be there forever. I would disregard the European convention and spend a full fourteen hours flogging the stream as if there were no tomorrow — which turned out to be the case. This daydream day, however, is not so much of a dream as it may appear. I am scrupulous in my fantasies, and every part of the day we are about to spend fishing this river of memory occurred at least once to me on actual fishing days.

In the first place, I would not lie abed and then enjoy a leisurely breakfast as I once did because I have to pack everything into this one day. I'd ask for a seven-o'clock breakfast which would be served to me with raised eyebrows but with politeness. Admittedly, this is not a desperate hour of the day for an American trout fisherman in mid-summer, but on the Traun it would have caused discussion. Was I an eccentric or merely an insomniac? No matter. I would be on the water two hours ahead of any other angler and the weir pool, less than a hundred yards from the inn door, would be mine exclusively until I hooked or landed the most eager fish, at least.

This pool started with a roaring, narrow chute of water, concentrated enough to run the full 150-foot length of the short pool with slack water and return eddies on both sides. For this heroic water I put on a light salmon leader tapered to OX, or about eight-pound test, decorated with a large #4 Grey Ghost streamer. I cast this quartering into the choppy current and when it has swung into the slower water retrieve it with short twitches. These trout have never seen an American streamer fly before (Europeans use large, fancy Scotch salmon flies for this type of angling) and the sleek, sinuous profile of this famous smelt imitation is more than these fish can resist. Every few casts I get a bruising strike. Hooked fish play hard and deep, threatening to run out of the pool, and it is only when they are quite tired that they can be urged into the quieter water and played back up toward the dam I am standing on. Unfortunately, a small tree, the relic of a spring flood, is wedged up under the apron and the tiring fish head for this sanctuary with their last ounce of strength. I can control fish up to three pounds or so easily, but some dreadnaughts cruise relentlessly into this snag and I have to break them off by hand, wondering if that might have been the fish to beat the local record of a shade over seventeen pounds.

One morning I hooked seven fish here and lost them all at the last minute. The *Fischmeister*, Hans Gebetsreither, was watching this performance from a window in the kitchen where he was enjoying his morning cup of coffee, and he marched down to the dam to see what was going on. He tested my leader and gave a grudging grunt as the tough monofilament nearly cut his hand and then swished my stiff eight-foot rod, which had killed several salmon in Canada, and shook his head in disgust. "When you are with a salmon fly-fishing you should also a salmon-rod be using," he said, or words to that effect. My German is a low-grade pidgin at best, but Hans's guttural grumbling was easy to translate: "Stop butchering my lovely fish with that Mickey-Mouse rod. Instantly." I skulked downriver to more open, snag-free water.

The fish I had been hooking—and mostly losing—here were mainly *Forelle* or brown trout, but some were the green-backed, silver-sided *Seeforelle* (lake trout) and once in a while a leaping *Lachsforelle* (salmon trout). The *Seeforelle* were flashier fighters than the regular, yellow-bellied browns, but were probably relatives that had recently drifted down from the lake above where they had been enjoying a different diet and habitat. *Lachsforelle*, however, puzzle me to this day. The Europeans who fished here said they were a true landlocked salmon, and their love of fast water and habit of leaping when hooked made a strong case for this parentage. On the other hand, no salmon of any kind are native to the Danube watershed, of which the Traun is a part, and the black spots on the backs and sides of these silvery fish were too large for salmon. Whatever their exact ancestry, they certainly fought like landlocks every inch of the way.

By now it is 9:30. I am running out of streamer flies and ready-taking fish so I head for the stretch of pocket-water below the tail of the weir pool. It is still too early for hatching flies and rising trout, so I change to a #10 wet fly, say a gold-ribbed Hare's Ear, and fine my leader down to 3X. I have had a lot of exercise above and decide to fish in the lazy man's manner for a while, letting the fly swing down-current on a quartering line and taking a step downriver after each presentation.

Every ten casts or so there is either a thump on the rod or a yowl from the reel, or both, and a fish runs down-current. Wading is slow and treacherous in this stretch, and I lose most of the fish trying to bring them back up-current. These are browns in the one-to-three-pound category, but they fight like full-grown grilse in this fast water.

I am through the pockets and into the flat below by 10:30 and I have been noticing rising fish working below me in the slow, deep water. Now I have to go back to work again, and I follow the path to the foot of this flat, add a 4X tippet, and rummage through my box for a likely imitation of the dark dun I have seen hatching. A #12 Quill Gordon doesn't seduce many fish so I change to a #14 Red Quill and the fishing picks up. These are chalkstream conditions; weedy bottom, slow, deep water that calls for snail-like wading and delicate presentation. These trout are all browns, mostly near the 16-inch limit with a few larger ones thrown in for excitement, but this is the Lilliputian fishing of the day. It is as rewarding as it is demanding, though, and an hour of fishing of this quality on the Battenkill or Beaverkill back home would make a "remember the time when . . ." story to be told and retold.

Just before noon I head up to the weir again, cross over to the left side of the current on the small catwalk, walk out on the bar

A three-pound *Lachsforelle*, the mystery fish of the Traun. At twenty-one inches, it was just barely a keeper.

formed below the plunge-pool, and face up-current. On this side of the main spillway current there are more than a dozen small rivulets formed by leaks in the weir-boards that bubble into minipools just below the dam-apron. The air temperature is nearly eighty degrees by now and there's a blazing sun overhead so I don't expect to see fish rising. I must pound them up with a variant. I put on a ginger-and-grizzley that's as big as a silver dollar and start prospecting the tail end of the poollet on the extreme right, extending each new cast up closer to the bubbles at the head.

The drag here is tricky and in some trickles I do nothing, but I raise a couple of fish in some of the bigger ones. In all, I raise eight fish, hook six, and land four from fourteen to eighteen inches — all browns. This is a modest showing. I once took ten from these same runnels in forty-five minutes before going in to lunch.

The midday meal is served with choice of beer or wine and is topped off with fresh fruit or berries and a selection of the world's great cheeses. It is perfect weather for a midday nap. There are also several afternoon performances of operas, concerts, and plays in Salzburg, one of the world's few great small cities, only fifty minutes away. But this is to be an all-fishing day, a maximum effort.

I get my tackle into the car and drive four or five miles downstream to a long, sandy-bottomed flat below an old mill. There are very few trout here but there are schools of grayling, pale grey shadows fanning the sand with their pectoral fins waiting for food to pass overhead. They are only partly competitive with trout; they live in different water and eat midges and small insects that the trout usually consider beneath their dignity. I go down to a 5X leader with a #18 black nymph and slowly prospect down-current. I miss my first hit—these fish shoot straight up from the bottom and are back down in a wink—and decide to stay put, for these are usually school fish. I get no more hits on the nymph so I wade thirty feet downstream and spot the school not twenty feet away when one of them rises. Grayling are much less shy than trout and will rise to your fly even when they can see you clearly, but they are choosy feeders and hard to hook. I put on a dark #18 dry fly and that's just what they've been waiting for. I get hit after hit, hooking every other fish that rises, till the school finally catches on and moves away. They were

A lovely flat, down-river from the inn, where grayling up to three pounds rose steadily under the afternoon sun.

typically all of a size, 12 to 13 inches in this group, and put up a reasonable fight although not as long and strong-hearted as a trout's. They are beautiful fish in the hand, though, sweet-smelling with a few black specks on their silverish sides, lavender backs and long, soft dorsal fins that try to convince you these are freshwater sailfish.

I run through two more schools on my way down the pool before I spot a large solitary fish lying between two patches of weed. It could be just a chub, yet it might be the grayling I'm hoping for. I cover him with the small dry fly and up he comes with the flash of purple that says grayling. The first two minutes of fight are vigorous enough, and then he comes in like an old shoe and I am disappointed with his lack of stamina. This is only July, though, and the big spring spawners aren't back into fighting shape yet, I have been told. In October they are something else and Charles Ritz rates them better than trout in their own proper season. Anyway, this fish is just a hair under twenty inches and the best one I have taken to date.

It's five o'clock and early dinner will be available in an hour, so I decide to finish off the afternoon with a few trout. With no shadows falling across the river yet, my only chance seems the plunge-pool below the old mill just above the grayling flat. I prospect the bubbly edge of the fast water here with the big variant again, raising six and landing three in the next half-hour. The shadows finally start to creep towards me from the far bank and I have to make a difficult decision: Should I continue fishing or head back for an early supper and enjoy more of the late-evening fishing? I hate to leave, but I know my chances for really large fish are better once the sun is down. I head for my car to make the short run back to the inn.

By 7:30, somewhat rested and refreshed by an *apéritif* and a cold supper, I walk up the formal promenade path that lines this portion of the bank to the very head of the river, nearly half a mile up-current where the water pours out of the lake through sturdy gates. It's a pleasant walk in the cool of the evening, and since I won't need waders the stroll can be made in the comfort of sneakers and slacks. Couples sitting on the benches murmur "Petri Heil," giving me the best wishes of our patron saint. The proper reply, I have learned, is "Petri dank."

To go fishing again after all the trout and grayling I have raised, hooked, and either lost or caught seems gluttonous, but this is to be a day remembered for a lifetime and it would be unthinkable to miss the *crescendo* of large fish and frenzied rising that will occur as darkness settles. First, though, I will warm up on medium-sized fish, cast to in a leisurely manner.

The narrow rush of water into the wide riverbed here causes curling counter-eddies on both edges where unseen fish rise like small minnows, poking their noses up into patches of foam for trapped insects. I have fished here only once before and on that occasion Hans, the *Fischmeister*, rigged me with two medium-sized wet flies which he told me to cast straight across the counter-current to float dead drift, and then to dance the dropper for a second or two before retrieving once drag had set in. Since I am standing three or four feet above river level this latter maneuver is easy to execute—even though it's nearly impossible when you're waist-deep in the water.

This is easy fishing from an eagle's vantage point, and I begin to wonder whether or not a spent-wing dry fly will work better when the rod is wrenched downward sharply and then flies back up. My point fly is gone and it's all my fault, but I was using a 2X leader and had felt that such a hefty tippet was plenty of insurance. Not with these fish, though. The ones I hooked or saw last time ranged from two to six pounds and they darted back to their lies desperately when hooked in this slow water.

I re-rig and pay more attention to my work. In several minutes I am into another and give line quickly enough this time. When I have the fish under control just below my feet, I realize I've made another mistake. Without a guide or long-handled net, how can I get this three-pound *Seeforelle* up a sheer masonry wall more than three feet high? I try to handline the trout up to the rail, but he wakes up and kicks off halfway to the top. I continue fishing, luckily landing one slightly smaller fish and being wound around underwater pilings by two far bigger fish that took control from the start.

My watch tells me I have ten minutes to cross over and meet Tony, the assistant *Fischmeister*, nearly a quarter of a mile downstream, for the last pitch of the day—awesome fishing for huge trout that go bump in the night. I reel in and "Petri dank" my way downriver to an old pier that juts out a dozen feet or more into the slowed river.

Tony is there rigging up new leaders, sturdier ones of about 1X with #14 dry caddis imitations on the point and on the dropper. He knots one onto my line and keeps two spares handy. After a break you can't risk a light on this water to tie on new flies, but whole rigged leaders can be attached by feel.

It's 8:30 and I sit there with my feet dangling just above the water, resting up for the grand finale. This will be the slowest fishing of the day. I will get only two or three hits in the coming hour of painstaking casting and feeling my flies gliding over the water, but this will be my chance for the biggest dry-fly trout of a lifetime. It isn't pleasant fishing, though, or even very interesting. It is simply trout fishing on a scale that I may never see again.

When it is finally too dark to tie on a fly, something brushes my face and then I feel a tickle in my hair. It's starting. I look up at the sky directly overhead and see a few, then several and, finally, many tiny forms hurrying with batlike, erratic flight through the

An Austrian *Fischmeister* with leather knickers, national hat, and a bring-'em-back-alive *Lagl* heavy with fish and water.

air. The caddis are up and a glance across the leadlike surface of the pool shows me that the trout are, too. Small dimples appear everywhere as if someone had scattered a handful of birdshot across the water. I am not fooled by the dainty, dace-like quality of the rise-forms, though, for I have been here before at this time of day — or is it night? These are usually huge fish up from the fifteen-to-twenty-foot depths for their only outing of the day.

I screw down the drag on my oversized trout reel as fast as it will go and start stripping line from the spool. There's no need to cast far. There are enough fish rising within twenty to thirty feet of me to fill a barrel. I shoot my team of dry flies twenty-five feet straight across the stream and strain my eyes to follow their progress on the surface. They move so slowly that when they start to drag they leave no wake, but merely cruise in toward the shore below me. Each cast takes a minute or two — it seems like much more — to fish out and then I repeat the procedure. These fish are old and wise and make very few mistakes even in pitch-darkness.

In a few minutes I am casting like an automaton, my arm making the prescribed motions every minute or so, but my mind is elsewhere. Tony is waiting patiently, standing at my left shoulder, uttering occasional phrases of encouragement, but my German is too weak for any sustained conversation. When my mind has finally drifted several thousand miles away, my line slowly grows tight, as if it has caught a snag, and I give the rod a twitch to free it by reflex action. Damn! There aren't any snags out there. I have just pulled the fly out of the mouth of the evening's first unwise fish. I reel in, Tony patiently feels the flies to be sure all is still in order, and I start casting again.

Fifteen minutes later I am napping so deeply that a fish is on before my tired reflexes can betray me. I raise my rod-tip and apply all the pressure I dare, but without result. The reel gives up line with short, grudging grunts, and if I didn't know better I would be certain I had hooked into a rowboat passing by in the dark. A short while after I feel the line-to-backing splice slip through my fingers, the procession comes to a halt, but I still feel the slow, steady throb of the fish's tail telegraphed up the line. Then, after a minute or so, all I can sense is the steady pull of the current.

I hand the rod to Tony. He plucks the tight line like a bass-fiddle string, pulls hard from several angles and then I hear him reeling in. Miraculously, he ties on another fully rigged leader and the rod is back in my hands again. I glance at the radium dial of my wristwatch and see that it's 9:45—only a quarter-hour of legal fishing time left.

Again I cast out into the nothingness and stand there listening to the soft sound of fish sucking in flies. I am determined to concentrate and not spoil my last chance of the day. I have no notion of where my flies are. Am I waiting too long between casts, or not long enough to fish the presentation out? No matter, really. Each swing must pass over a dozen fish or more and I must wait for the law of averages to catch up with some trout.

It does, just before quitting time. This fish starts off more rapidly at first, then stops and shakes his head for a while and continues on majestically again. This time I'm in touch for a full five minutes and then the line comes back to me. At least I wasn't wound around a snag by this fish. The flashlight shows a straightened hook on the dropper fly. The first time I had been too gentle and on the second try I had been too heavy-handed. Or were these fish meant to remain uncaught? Tony says they land one occasionally, but that the chances are better slightly upriver and near the opposite shore. There are fewer boulders and snags there, and it can be fished from an anchored boat. Perhaps I would like to try there tomorrow evening? I agree to the plan even though I know tomorrow will never come. We have a cold beer together back at the inn, then I bid him a drowsy goodnight. I am bone-weary and half asleep.

How many fish have I hooked this day? I try to tally up the number of rises, fish hooked, and fish landed. I was into at least fifty, probably nearer to a hundred including the grayling. I landed less than half of them, though, and very few of the big ones. Too tired to make an exact accounting, I head upstairs to bed. I feel sure, though, that I have had a larger poundage of fish on my line during this one day than I might hook into during an entire season back home on northeastern waters.

Admittedly, this was a daydream day — a composite patched together from the best parts of other days I had enjoyed on the lower Traun. Even so, such a day had been a possibility. How could fishing be so good? This was no mountain wilderness. The Traun valley had been settled, farmed, lived in for a dozen centuries or more and it had even played host to a certain amount of industrial development. For example, the weir across from the inn backed up water for both a local brewery and a small textile mill and yet the water was returned to the river in "troutable"—if not quite potable—condition.

This land had become populated gradually and lovingly. There had been no sudden housing developments or rush of industrial exploitation in this area. As the population grew, safeguards on water usage and sewage treatment had been written and enforced *before* any damage could be done.

That the river was pure enough for trout was due to one type of planning, but that doesn't explain the size and the number of trout. This was the result of a fishery-management policy that ensured good fishing for native species without any necessity for stocking. In fact, it is hard to imagine that the fishing here had possibly been any better a hundred, five hundred, or even a thousand years ago. The harvest was in perfect balance with production.

The size limits I mentioned earlier had a little to do with this, but several other rules, written and unwritten, safeguarded this fishery. First, and perhaps most important, was a limit on the number of fishing permits issued per day. These cost about $3 per day or $12 for a full week back in 1960 — a modest sum, but enough to keep all but serious anglers off the water in those days. More important, the limited number of permits kept the water from being overfished and the fish from being harassed to the point where they'd hide during the day and rise only at dusk. I am convinced that the brown trout's reputation for being a night-feeder is due to his being stepped on by an army of anglers during daylight hours on our most popular public rivers and that fish would feed far more steadily during daylight hours if there were less traffic.

Second, anglers here paid for every fish they kept. The price was about three-quarters of the open market price for trout (wild fish *can* be sold in most parts of Europe) so that few fish were kept for bragging purposes. If you wanted a fish for a meal you kept

Looking down-river from the dam beside the inn. This section of the river alone could have kept an angler happy for life.

one, and the smallest keeping-size trout here (16 inches) made a hearty meal.

Lastly, anglers didn't carry off crates of iced fish with them when their time was up. Whether this was an aspect of the law or merely a tradition I never found out. Countless fisheries in Canada have been skimmed down to mediocrity by anglers who insisted on taking coolers and crates of iced fish back home with them. Anglers on the Traun might take a fish or two with them if they were within a day's trip of home, but there was no wholesale haulage, and I'm sure any guest who tried this—even though the catch was legally paid for — would subsequently find the inn booked solid no matter how far ahead he called in his reservation.

When a dam was built downriver from the Marienbrucke fishery several years ago, it backed up the water and flooded this stretch, destroying a showcase fishery for all the world to wonder at and imitate. The power dam may have been an economic necessity for the region, but the world is the poorer for it. And dams are like taxes: They never disappear, they only increase.

Perhaps we can never have a Traun-like fishery in this country. The rich though cool lake water that fed it might be hard to duplicate, but we might get three-quarters of the way there by following some easy examples. We could make sure the water used by local industry is returned to a river with trout-tolerable quality. We could raise our size-limits. And we could limit the number of fish taken. And just possibly, a few enlightened years from now, we could limit traffic on a few showcase stretches by issuing permits in a limited number on a lottery basis so that anglers who really cared might see free-rising trout all day long for at least a few days each season. I don't know how state conservation departments would react to this last suggestion. But I do know a lot of fishermen who would stand in line a long time for the chance to fish quality water like that, and I am one of them.

# 11

# The Ultimate Fly Rod

Men are emotional about fly rods. Trout rods in particular, yet perhaps even about the hefty rods used in salt water for bonefish and tarpon, or about freshwater rods used for bass bugging and streamer fishing. Men may love a salmon rod. But light, split-cane fly rods are objects of reverence. A Payne, Halstead, Gillum, Garrison, Leonard, Orvis, Winston, Young, Thomas, or an Edwards trout rod may well be the most cherished piece of equipment used in any sport.

The only serious rival is the wing shooter's fine double shotgun. In fact, fly rod and shotgun have much in common. Both are used in the beauty of the wild outdoors. And both become intimate extensions of the body in motion. In some respects, though, the fly rod is the more intimate companion. It seems to be alive. It bends and moves in response to the angler's touch. The rod is a more constant friend, too. Fishing seasons are longer than shooting seasons, and, while a bird shooter may fire several times in a day afield, the trouter will number his casts in the thousands.

Add to this the fact that a day on his favorite stream is a semireligious experience for the dedicated angler. The trout stream is set apart from other scenes of sport—by hemlock and rhododendron, willow and warbler, the play of sunlight on a riffle. Many fine authors have tried to capture this magic, but it beggars description. A great naturalist once described a stream as "the artery of the forest." It is that and more. It is also the life blood of the trouter.

In this setting and in this spirit, a rod becomes far more than just a tool for casting. And, fortunately, this bond between rod and man is an especially happy one. The experienced angler seldom blames his rod. In fact, he is all too liable to consider it perfection.

This happiness with things as they are can be observed in almost any fine tackle store. There are seldom requests for unconventional rod actions or special embellishments. If you examine a sampling of rods by the finest makers, you will see that they are almost uniformly modest in appearance. The brown cane glows warmly through the clear varnish. The reel seat is a harmonious cedar or walnut. Windings will usually be a neutral tan. This is the quiet beauty of the partridge, not the gaudy beauty of the cock pheasant.

And yet, despite the generic description above, each maker subtly signs his own work. Custom-made reel fittings differ from one another. The shape of the cork grip often indicates the maker. And then there's the cane itself. Most Leonards are quite light-colored. So are Garrisons and Gillums. Paynes are medium-brown. Halsteads and Orvises are quite dark brown.

Any of these fine rods is fairly expensive. One may cost from $200 to perhaps slightly more than $350. But it is definitely not a rich man's plaything, or a status symbol. A great many of these rods are in the hands of people of very modest means. I once saw a farmer fishing with a Gillum in the stream that ran behind his barn. When I admired the rod he looked a bit sheepish and admitted, "I've always wanted one of these, and then I made a bit of extra money trapping last winter. But my wife sure doesn't know how much I paid for it." You can be sure that many lunches have been skimped or skipped in order to pay for a dream rod.

Is a $250 bamboo rod ten times as good as a $25 glass rod? There's no pat answer. It all depends on your sense of values.

The recently deceased Everett Garrison, one of the very finest custom makers, defended his art with some science. "A glass rod doesn't throw the smooth curve of line that a fine bamboo does. Stop-motion photography proves this." All well and good, but why do most tournament distance casters now use glass? "It's a very powerful material, all right," Garrison admitted. "But they haven't got the tapers worked out yet. Perhaps some day."

There's more to it than that. There's a "sweet feel" to a great bamboo rod that just can't be duplicated. When you're casting thousands of times a day, this advantage may be worth a lot in pure enjoyment—even if it won't catch more fish. A bamboo rod should last the average fisherman at least twenty years. That comes to $12.50 per year. When you look at it that way, a great rod isn't an extravagance.

There's a joker in that twenty-year life expectancy, though. It's only a median figure. A rod may last a man a lifetime if he fishes only several times a year. On the other hand, the screen door has ended the life of many a rod before it delivered its first cast. Each year hundreds of fine rods are crushed underfoot, splintered against tree trunks, or chopped off by car doors. Surprisingly, rod breakage while actually playing a trout is one of the rarest forms of disaster.

Perhaps it isn't fair to measure a rod's life in terms of years. Barring accidents, it should be measured in numbers of casts. For each time a bamboo rod flexes, it dies a little. It may take years to notice a change in power and action, for an angler unwittingly suits his casting style to the rod in hand. But fatigue is inexorable. The finest, steeliest dry-fly rod I ever owned — or ever handled for that matter — was an eight-foot Halstead. I still own it and cherish it, but I seldom fish with it. After some seven hundred and fifty days of dogged dry-fly fishing, it's a slow, lazy parody of its former self.

All great rods don't die; some escape both catastrophe and senility. But they survive in collections, like pinned insects, as a matter of record. In one notable collection is a priceless "gold" rod. Its history belongs to a brasher era, when the president of a kerosene company (which grew into Standard Oil) refused to be outdone by royalty. When this captain of industry heard that Queen Victoria had a rod with all-gold fittings, he decided to match her. He commissioned America's top rodmaker to make him a rod with all-gold ferrules and reel seat — then had all the metal intricately engraved by the finest gun engraver of the day!

In the same collection is a more modest, yet more historic rod.

It was the favorite of Theodore Gordon, who, before his death in 1915, pioneered and established dry-fly fishing in America. The many excellent rods of the great Edward R. Hewitt seemed to have escaped the collectors, even though Hewitt died less than two decades ago. His grandchildren don't know where they all went. Have they fallen unceremoniously into the hands of the great-grandchildren? I hate to think that these rods might be suffering the same fate as my grandfather's ten-foot Thomas. I well remember using it with a quarter-ounce sinker, fishing for flounders off Cape Ann, Massachusetts, when I was a larcenous and untutored eight-year-old.

Sadly, great rods are being ruined or retired faster than they are being built. Demand for the very finest easily exceeds supply in our affluent society.

One hundred years ago, production was also negligible. The ardent angler made his own rods and perhaps a few extras for his friends; these rods of ash, lancewood, or greenheart, while finely finished and ferruled, were relatively simple in construction. Rod guides were often simple unbraced rings which flopped as the line struggled through. Samuel Phillippe changed all this.

The art of lamination had been used in older bows; in the early nineteenth century, English rod tips of three-part design were used, and some glued work must have appeared then. Phillippe was an Easton, Pennsylvania, gunsmith who fished. He made violins as well. With the skill of a minor Stradivarius, he revolutionized the trout rod.

What was probably the first entire split-cane rod appeared in America in 1848 — Phillippe's "rent and glued-up cane" rod, as it was called then. He wisely chose the six-part, hexagonal cross-section, which offers a flat, glued plane for flexion. Nine-, eight-, five-, and four-segment rods would be tried and discarded.

Phillippe's son, Solon, and later Charles Murphy, learned from the master. In 1870, the great self-taught builder Hiram L. Leonard began varnishing wonderful rods in Bangor, Maine. Thomas, Edwards, and the elder Edward Payne, whose son James became the finest rodbuilder who has ever touched a plane, learned at Leonard's bench.

George Parker Holden, a hobbyist and writer on rods many

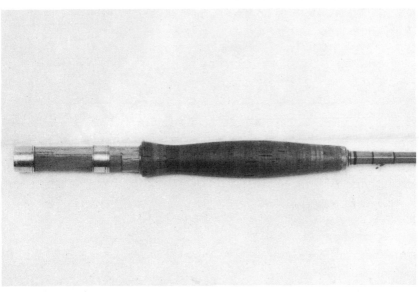

Close-up of typical Leonard trout-rod hardware. Grip shape is not standard, but light-colored reel seat and slip ring are.

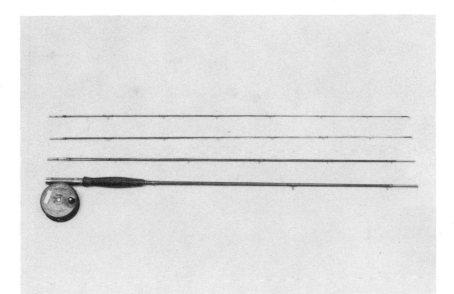

Nine-foot trout rod from Leonard. Windings are usually brighter and bamboo tone lighter than somber, monotone Paynes.

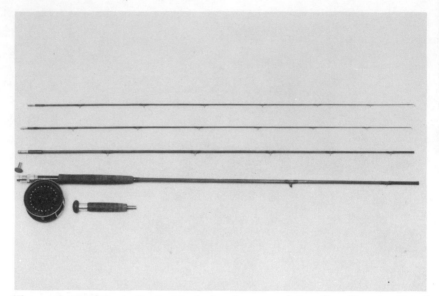

Ten-and-a-half-foot single-handed salmon rod by Jim Payne. Small butt-plug pulls out, extension is inserted for playing fish.

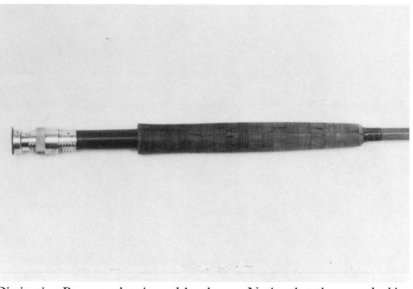

Distinctive Payne cork grip and hardware. Notice that the screwlocking mechanism is at rear, keeping reel near grip.

years ago, made his own, and trained Everett Garrison, an architect, to build by fits and starts for the custom trade.

But one day several years ago, Jim Payne told a friend, "I'm leaving the shop, I don't know when I'll be back." He died a month later. The announcement of his death in the New York papers precipitated a run on Abercrombie & Fitch's stock of used Payne rods — his output had been low for years. Paynes have doubled in price; the big salmon rods, which he stopped making about twenty years ago, are worth $750, prime condition, against $150. Younger hands struggle to keep the Payne shop going. Pinkey Gillum, Payne's fine apprentice, who built rods independently for years, had been dead for nearly a decade when Jim Payne left the shop for the last time. Nat Uslan, who also learned from Payne, retired a few years ago. Edwards, Thomas, and Garrison have all died. The masters are not being replaced.

The Charles Orvis Company in Manchester, Vermont, must be credited with offering the contemporary angler a fine rod on the retail rack. Their 2,500 pieces a year, along with the production of Young of Detroit, Winston of San Francisco, and Leonard of Orange County, New York, barely touch present demand, despite the inroads of glass. Very little that is wonderful is coming out of England or France, and the Japanese seem to have failed as rodmakers.

What makes one rod great, another mediocre? Materials and workmanship. The trout rod is pared to an irreducible minimum, a trend that began when the dry-fly method reached fad proportions under Theodore Gordon's tutelage in the early 1900s. False casting, short float, and recasting made the old ten-foot rods instruments of torture after an hour or so of fishing. Builders competed for lightness by sixteenths of an ounce. While the salmon rod remained a symphony, the dry-fly rod became a quartet. The slightest flaw in taper or action is quickly transmitted to the hand. The real devotee pursues his jewel-sided quarry with bamboo; glass is rare in the top trout clubs.

Bamboo, the muscle and sinew of the rod, is a large grass of which there are many species, sizes, and qualities. The first rods —perhaps Phillippe's original rods—were built of Calcutta bamboo. Today this is porch-furniture bamboo, not rod material.

Modern rods are built of what is called Tonkin bamboo, said to be found only in a small area in southern China. One legend has it that only those stalks that grow on the hilltops are first rate, because they have been strengthened by resisting the wind. Another story is that this bamboo has ceased to exist in a wild state and is a cultivated crop. Most likely, there are several species of bamboo that have the desired strength and straightness for rod building.

A store of well-aged and dried canes of this type is the rodmaker's bank account. They are eight feet long, three inches in diameter, and may have cost only $2 apiece. They are the first key to quality, as is the stock of hackle necks or a particular strain of live roosters to a fly-tyer.

But even a plentiful supply of the best cane is no assurance of perfect materials, for individual canes must be specifically selected for special tasks. Here a knowledge of the microscopic construction of bamboo and how it works is essential. A cross-section of a piece of bamboo reveals small, powerful fibers that run the length of the section of cane and are embedded in a relatively neutral, but binding, matrix. A closer examination of this cross-section reveals that these fibers are very close together on the outside of the cane, or nearest the exterior enamel, and that they become less and less dense as you approach the pithier interior.

A rodmaker examines this cross-section very carefully as he selects a cane for a particular purpose. If he is going to build a seven-and-a-half-foot dry-fly rod, he looks for a cane with a dense cluster of fibers on the outside edge. He may have to examine and discard several canes to find this type. On the other hand, he may find one with an exceptionally dense power structure running well into the interior. This is a special prize, but not for the seven-and-a-half-foot trout rod. This cane he marks and puts away for use in a larger, more powerful salmon rod.

Only when a suitable cane has been selected from an already highly-selected batch of bamboo can the work proper commence. This consists of turning a single piece of cane into a fly rod of several sections, each of which is made up of six separate but absolutely equal slices of bamboo. While this fact of hexagonal structure is widely known, it is also often the sum total of an angler's knowledge about bamboo rods — even among men who own several of the finest. Yet, this is about the same as a sports-car driver knowing only that cars have four wheels!

Actually, the hand-making of a fine rod is part art, part craftsmanship, and it is a lengthy and painstaking process. Here are some of the major steps involved in the order that some, but not all, rodmakers follow.

First, the selected cane is split in half and the partitions inside each node are cut out with a gouge. If the rod is to be the popular seven-and-a-half-footer, in two pieces and with an extra tip, one half is split into six equal sections and put aside for the butt section. The other half is split into twelve pieces for the two tips. The pieces forming each section are cut and arranged with nodes staggered so that no two fall opposite each other. Pieces are numbered so they can be reassembled in the same sequence.

Each piece is then placed in a V former, and the two split sides planed to an angle. The nodes, which protrude slightly on the enamel side, are then filed approximately flush, and now the eighteen strips are ready for straightening. If the bamboo had been sawed into strips — as is the case with many high-quality rods made by larger concerns — this step would not be necessary. But Tonkin cane grows straight once in a blue moon; normally, split-cane sections veer off a few degrees at each node, and it is at these awkward natural joints that the rodmaker sets to work.

Fortunately, bamboo has very plastic qualities when heated to a certain, rather high temperature. By holding the node over a small lamp and turning it carefully to prevent burning or charring, bamboo may be straightened by applying moderate pressure, and the strip will hold its shape after it has cooled.

The straightened strips are then heat-treated to give them the extra steely quality that even well-seasoned cane does not possess. It would be easier to do this baking after they had been planed to size, but the process causes some shrinkage that might make the final rod thinner than planned. It is best to heat-treat before planing even though the extra hardness will make the planing a bit more difficult.

Hours of this delicate work make all the pieces of each section alike to within one-thousandth of an inch. The strip is placed into a V form which has caliper adjustments every several inches; all pieces comprising that section are cut flush to the form. Only two sides of the strip may be worked on. A cut off one side. Turn the strip. A cut off the other. Near the end of this process, the enamel, which has no power, is removed with one clean stroke. No further planing on the rind side is permissible on a fine rod.

From the artisan's point of view, the rod is now done; its final action and feel have been fully imprinted into the bamboo. Of course, there are many hours of work left: glueing and pressure-winding the strips, trueing them up, seating of the ferrules, fitting the grip and reel seat, winding and fixing the guides, and three coats of varnish. But though it must be meticulously done, all this is journeyman's work.

A top rodmaker says it takes him a minimum of twenty-five hours to make a rod. Working hours—not counting the hours and days he must wait for glue or varnish to set. I think he's underestimating his labor considerably.

When you consider that the top custom-made trout rods sold for as little as $100 only ten years ago, the economics of fine rodmaking seem incredible. Without figuring in the rent, the materials, or the tools, the finest craftsmen in the field were probably making less than $4 an hour!

But these are proud and devoted men. You stand in line for a rod. Often you have to wheedle and cajole. I know one board chairman of a huge company who waited a year and a half for his nine-foot salmon rod. Finally he called the rodmaker and approached the matter with tact. He was told, "I haven't had time to start it yet. I'll call you when it's ready."

Another builder, troubled by telephone interruptions, calmly ripped the old-fashioned receiver off the wall and went on about his business.

It was a fine, monastic life, at $4 an hour.

The trade cannot possibly survive; but the rods, and the tradition, do.

# Dream Tackle

Although I may be too old to believe in the Tooth Fairy, I am not yet so calloused by the years that I can't enjoy my own grown-up gift fantasies. One of my favorite daydreams starts with an imaginary rich relative telling me to pick out for myself the two finest fly-fishing outfits I can find — regardless of cost. Sensibly enough, one is to be for trout fishing and the other, a bit heftier, for Atlantic salmon and the like. There is only one condition: this must be tackle I will fish with regularly, not museum or elaborate presentation pieces that might be resold for a mint.

Outside of that there are no strings attached and no obligations. This is important. Since I can't pay for this gear and I can't profit by reselling it, I won't be snatching the bread from the hungry mouths of my children. I can even assemble the rods and swish them fondly through the air right in front of my wife without the tiniest twinge of guilt. The advantages of this particular wish-fulfillment game are enormous and it beats counting sheep when you're tossing and turning in bed.

Have you got the rules straight now? Then put your money away and let's go shopping.

We'll look at rods first. Reels are not nearly as important and should be matched to the particular rod chosen, anyway. Lines, too, must fit the rod and with the new AFTM numbering system and the many excellent floaters and sinkers now on the market, this will be the easiest part of the game.

Since money is no object, I will look at bamboo rods only. This is not snobbery or affectation. I know that good fiberglass and graphite rods will cast farther per ounce of rod, and when I'm occasionally granted a third outfit for saltwater work one of these easily comes in first. But for ninety-nine percent of all freshwater fly-fishing, sheer distance is not the first consideration. Synthetic fiber rods are also more durable and virtually maintenance-free but these qualities don't turn my stubborn head, either. I don't mind the extra task of wiping bamboo dry and caring for it after fishing any more than I feel put upon when I clean and oil-wipe a fine shotgun. Come to think of it, I rather enjoy the ritual.

No, the reason why I will choose split-cane rods for both outfits is that they are not only lovelier to look at, but they are sweeter in the hand than any others and they seem to present a fly more delicately. Why this is so I cannot explain or prove. Perhaps it's because they are solid instead of hollow. Perhaps it's because split cane is a living, organic material. (After all, fine leather feels better than vinyl, rubbed wood better than plastic.) Or it may be that the finest bamboo rods have been tapered and tailored with an artistry that mass-produced synthetics can never capture. If you've ever fished with a great split-cane rod you'll know what I mean, and perhaps you can explain the difference to yourself.

My choice of length for a trout rod will surprise you only if you haven't read Chapter 7. I will want something between eight and nine feet. Shorter rods may be interesting conversation pieces and even quite adequate for specialized situations, but I'd never choose one for all-around trout fishing. A rod of that length would make me work too hard to cover the river and, more important, it would leave more line on the water, causing drag to set in much sooner after each presentation. I know from experience that ultra-short rods are more tiring, despite their lighter weight, and that they are inferior trout-catching tools.

On the other hand, a rod of over nine feet might seem superior for all the above reasons, but such is seldom the case. Really long single-handed rods can be tiring for the rapid-fire casting that's often necessary in trout fishing, and a bamboo rod that works best with a #5-weight line starts to lose its decisive, crisp action after a certain critical length. I have handled many delightful 8½-foot trout rods, and I'm pretty sure I can find exactly what I want in this length.

For salmon fishing I will want a longer, stronger rod, and since I won't be casting or false-casting nearly as frequently I'm sure I can handle one all day that measures from 9½ to 10½ feet. The longer rod will give me slightly better control of the speed of my fly when wet-fly fishing, and since I will only be making a cast every thirty seconds or so my arm won't complain. Another advantage of this longer rod over the now-popular eight-foot salmon stick is that it casts farther with less effort and will let me pull more line off the water for the back-cast without stripping in so many coils of line before the lift-off. While it can be argued that the short rod can cast just as far with the double-haul, casting is not the same as catching. You will spend much more time false-casting (and checking for leader knots!) and stripping in line for the lift-off than I will with my longer rod. My fly will be fishing the water and not flying through the air many more minutes each hour than yours will, and with the better line control and mending capabilities of the longer rod my fly will be traveling at the proper speed during more of each presentation, too.

There's only one drawback to my 10½-footer. When I change to a dry fly to cover a rolling fish I haven't been able to raise with a conventional wet, I will have to admit I have too much rod for this tactic. The frequent false-casting to dry the fly and the staccato presentations weary my arm in a few minutes. I can fish a 9½-footer with comfort this way, but it's not my ideal wet-fly rod. The great Edward R. Hewitt always used a 10½-footer for dry-fly, but he was made of sterner stuff than I am. How do I solve this wet-dry conflict? Compromise. A ten-footer gives excellent control for wet-fly fishing — which I find is about eighty to ninety percent of the fishing—and is also feasible for dry-fly work if I pace myself.

This ten-footer will have a lot of backbone, and I'm sure the maker would suggest an AFTM #9 or heavier for it, but I will match it with a selection of #7s and #8s. The reason for this is that I will be pulling forty feet or more of line off the water with its superior length and will false-cast fifty, sixty feet or more line in the air when wet-fly fishing. Since rodmakers estimate only thirty feet of line out beyond the tip in their calculations, my rod will be fully loaded with these lighter lines.

I have now decided on the lengths and strengths of my two ideal bamboo rods and that leaves only the brand or maker up for grabs. This is a ticklish situation since bamboo rods are as much individuals as people are, and no two, even of the same measurements by the same maker, are alike. Though several companies and makers are turning out excellent rods to this day, most of the superb ones I've handled came from a slightly earlier era. I'll probably choose a rod that was varnished during the golden age of American rodmaking—the '20s through the '50s.

Does this mean that with the whole world of rods to choose from, I'll end up with some second-hand stick? Well, yes, but let's not put it that way. If Cadillac can call a used car "previously owned," I can label my rods "previously cherished." Or look at it this way. Yehudi Menuhin and Jascha Heifetz aren't performing with brand-new fiddles, either. The violins they play are over two hundred years old and may have had dozens of previous owners.

Among rods of the great makers that I have seen and hefted, the ones by Jim Payne seem to have the edge on the average, and I think most fine-rod fanciers agree. Not only are they most beautiful to behold but their actions and feel are nearly always ultra-pleasing. An awkward or "sour" Payne is so scarce as to be a collector's item.

However, this is tackle for fishing, not for bragging, and I may end up with a Garrison, Gillum, Halstead, or even a rod by some lesser-known custom rodmaker. In fact, there's always the possibility that I'll be persuaded by a particularly choice rod by Thomas, Leonard, Orvis or one of the other excellent production companies past or present. But the percentages say I will end up with two Paynes that have had a lot of care and little fishing wear and tear, just as a concert violinist would probably choose a Stradivarius if he could take his pick from all the violins in the world.

We're coming down the home stretch now, with only reels to go, and again I find that we have just passed the pinnacle of design and workmanship. This is partly due to the confiscatory costs of hand-machining and partly to the current craze for ultra-lightness.

For a trout reel I can choose almost any model I want because I need one with some weight to counterbalance my 8½-foot rod. The Hardy Perfect reel, discontinued about ten years ago, will be my first choice. It is more reliable and can withstand more punishment than the lighter-frame reels being turned out today, and I know it will last me a lifetime and then some. I have seen fifty-year-old Perfects that have been used steadily and heavily and are even smoother than the late-production models. One with a 3⅝-inch diameter seems to balance best with my chosen rod and I know that, like a fine vintage wine, it will only get better in the next ten or twenty years.

Weight will not be an important consideration in choosing a salmon reel, either. In fact, one too light might tire my hand and cramp my fingers. I can think of four reels that are perfect for my ten-foot rod: the old Hardy Cascapedia, the Vom Hofe, the Zwarg, and the Walker. They all look alike, seem to be built on the same principles, and all are finely machined. Unfortunately, only the Walker is built today, so I might as well take one of their new ones. The size 2/0 balances my rod best and I prefer the model with a gearing advantage to take in line more rapidly.

Two Payne salmon rods: a rare twelve-foot, two-hander with a Vom Hofe reel (top) and a single-hander with Hardy Perfect.

Lines, as I've said, are easy to choose. I will need floaters, sinkers, and sinking-tip styles in size #5 for trout and size #7 (plus a few #8s for very windy days) for my salmon rod. I have no strong preference for any one brand among the top-quality plastic-line manufacturers. The good ones seem much alike to me. I will, however, also want a few silk lines that I can grease up for high floating and easy pick-up, and these are still being made in England.

And that's about it. I have now assembled the two finest fly-fishing outfits money can buy (or so I feel) and the good news is that money can, indeed, buy them. The rods and reels (minus the unspecified number of lines) could be picked up with a little hunting for about $1,000, and an astute or patient buyer might shave $100 or even more off this. Not a sumptuous sum really, when you consider that used private planes, sports cars, and fine shotguns come in at several times this much. This may be dream tackle, but it's a dream that's not so impossible if you can squirrel away a bit of cash after taxes.

So here we are now, back to the dream-game where this all started. It's an enjoyable game, as I've said, and there's even an ace-in-the-hole blessing to it. If, after shopping, comparing, buying, possessing, polishing, and assembling these outfits you still can't manage to get to sleep, be of good cheer. You can now start fishing the choicest sections of your favorite rivers and streams with this dream tackle, and if this secondary gambit doesn't lull you into slumber, so be it. Can you think of a more enjoyable way to spend a whole night of insomnia?

# 13

## The Deadliest Lure

There is a popular notion that flyfishermen are people who nobly impose an artificial handicap on themselves to make the catching of fish more difficult. But it just isn't so. Fly-fishing may be noble in its ideals; it is also devastatingly effective. In an appropriate form and properly fished, flies offer sport that cannot be duplicated by the wood or metal or plastic gadgetry of other lures.

Consider the evidence. For trout, the case is easy to build. Flies were originated to kill trout. The fragile aquatic insects which are the staple trout diet break up when skewered on a hook. Something more durable had to be created—and created it was, some two thousand years ago according to surviving records, and perhaps artificial flies were no novelty even then. The worm and the minnow may have their innings under certain conditions, but the fly is the most consistent trout killer and has been for centuries.

No less an authority than Edward R. Hewitt stated that the skillful nymph fisherman was the only man who could clean a stream of sophisticated brown trout by legal angling. And the nymph, though a fairly recent refinement, is very much a fly and in the classic tradition of close imitation.

Further proof is provided by the fact that professional fishermen use flies, perhaps not exclusively but very regularly. In

France, anglers who make a living by supplying restaurants with wild trout taken from heavily fished public streams use flies most of the time. In high water or when they're after a specific large fish, they may turn to the spun minnow, but they earn their daily French bread during most of the season with the fly. And I might add that the best of them may be the finest trout fishermen in the world.

The same is true in Spain. Men who fish the few public salmon rivers in the north use flies regularly when the water is neither too roily nor too deep. And when you consider that the average Spanish salmon can be sold for as much as a laborer earns in two months of hard work, you can be sure that the fly is no affectation there.

Trout and salmon may be the traditional victims of the fly, but all game fish, except perhaps those which live in unreachable depths, are highly susceptible to fur and feathers. Spinners, plugs, and naturals are not so universally effective, regardless of what their adherents may claim. New York State employs an expert fisherman to check populations of lakes, ponds, and streams and to catch fish for scale samples. His quarry are mainly smallmouth and largemouth bass, yet he uses a fly rod exclusively and claims that an orange streamer is his most effective lure.

Even commercial tuna fishermen in the Pacific use flies. For on the end of those two- and three-pole rigs with which they yank tuna into the boat there is a special quick-release hook covered with white feathers. And large white-feathered jigs have been used for decades by sport fishermen and commercial trollers.

Of course, the flies just described wouldn't be recognized as such under a New England covered bridge. Are, then, these large minnow and squid imitations really flies? In one sense yes, and in another no. The Spanish say no. They make a clear distinction that is surprising for a country not noted for its sport fishing. There, a fly that imitates an insect is properly called a *mosca*, while a streamer or salmon fly is a *pluma*. I think they are right in calling one the fly and the other the feathers, but our own language has no such nicety.

However, the English definition has its merits, too. Both the dainty insect imitation and the large feather squid owe their effectiveness to the same qualities — qualities that separate them

Modern minnow-imitating and attractor flies shown against a catalogue page picturing those of our grandfathers' era.

from the live bait, spinners, or solid wobbling plugs. First and foremost of these is the action of feather, fur, and hair. They breathe, wiggle, and kick in a unique manner when drawn through the water. And perhaps equally important, all these materials are translucent in the water, as are insects, minnows, elvers, or squid that they counterfeit.

In the beginning, of course, was the wet trout fly. In fact, until about a hundred years ago it was *the* fly. The great blossoming into many styles for many types of fishing is a rather recent development, and testifies to the high quality of the materials that flies are made of.

The artificial nymph, for instance, is merely a refinement of the basic wet fly, and it came out of England at the turn of the century. Probably the great Frederick Halford of dry-fly fame was indirectly responsible for its development, although he was to fight till his dying day against the use of nymphs. It was Halford who established the doctrine of exact mimicry in dry-fly fishing. So successful was he in implanting this ideal that wet-fly fishermen took to more exact imitation of the underwater, or nymphal, forms of aquatic insects. Under the leadership of G.E.M. Skues, the nymph fishermen fought the Halfordians for over a quarter of a century. While neither side ever won a clear-cut victory, the literature that resulted is some of the most spirited in the entire angling library. Since the turn of the century, the nymph has appeared in a wide variety of patterns. It is not only a recent invention but an extremely important one, for Hewitt was right in his estimate of its efficiency on wary fish such as the brown trout.

The streamer fly and its cousin the bucktail are purely American in origin. One story has it that a man was fishing with a large wet fly when the throat hackle broke, unwound, and streamed out behind the fly. This accidental lure was an immediate success and an idea was born. After all, big trout and landlocked salmon feed heavily on minnows, and a hackle feather of suitable color, undulating along the hook-shank, makes a very likely imitation, as we now know. However, the story is considered apocryphal. Officially, the streamer is credited to Maine fly-tyer Herb Welsh, and the date is recorded as 1901.

The bass fly was also developed in this country. In its older, purer forms, it is basically a huge trout-type wet fly, usually in one of the brighter patterns and dressed as fully as possible to make it a chunky mouthful. You don't see this type of fly around much any more, though. The big streamer fly has largely replaced it. And the exciting surface lures of clipped deer hair are becoming more popular each season. They mimic such delicacies of the bass menu as frogs, dragonflies, crayfish, and even mice. If hair-and-feather minnows and squid are to be considered flies, then these hair-bodied counterfeits would also seem to fit the category. And they do catch fish with gratifying regularity.

But unquestionably the most important fly development in recorded history is the dry fly. Here, too, there has been progress in recent years but, surprisingly, not because of any great advances in the science of entomology. Ronalds' *The Fly-fisher's Entomology* was published in England in 1836 and is still widely quoted. While it may be a taxonomist's horror (it avoids Latin names, preferring terms like Pale Watery Dun), it speaks the angler's language. In America we have no such single standard work. There have been valiant attempts like Ernest Schwiebert's *Matching the Hatch* and Art Flick's *Streamside Guide to Naturals and Their Imitations*. Schwiebert dealt with the entire United States, while Flick limited himself to New York's Catskills. Both books are often very useful. Yet I know a stream ecologically similar to Flick's Scoharie, and not forty miles from it, where half of the important insects bear no resemblance to Flick's favored dozen. Apparently, America is too huge, too rich, and too diverse a habitat for any one man to entomologize. This may be an argument in favor of the slight leaning toward impressionism discernible in many modern American flies.

There has also been a trend toward drabness, simply because drab flies seem to work well on our streams. No longer are flies designed primarily for brook trout in ponds, as they once were, because the ecological picture has changed. The colorful artificials which were used for that purpose evolved into bass flies.

Finally, there has been a trend toward chunky, less delicate dry flies on both sides of the Atlantic, and this has a simple explanation. Trout streams in most well-populated countries have a higher percentage of newly stocked fish each year. These trout must remember the hatchery mouthful better than the mayfly. They simply go for something which looks like an insect and is fat enough to rivet their attention. The highly selective wild brown trout of Halford's day are now hard to find, and today's flies reflect this change in conditions.

Furthermore, many more fish are considered game species now than in the late nineteenth century, and many more sportsmen have learned to use the fly rod. This has resulted in an incredible proliferation of both classic patterns and relatively new ones. Even if a fisherman finds himself on strange water with nothing to match the hatch precisely, he can switch from fly to fly until he finds a good one, or he can shop for local patterns. Being inexpensive, flies encourage experimentation.

Of course, certain of the oldest classic patterns are still with us in pretty much their original form — dries like the famous Blue Dun, wets like the Wickham's Fancy, Coachman, Leadwing Coachman, and Royal Coachman. They are far too effective to be forsaken. But excellence has not hindered experimentation. For instance, it was discovered quite early that some dry flies could be tied as wet patterns to imitate drowned insects. Hence, we have both wet and dry versions of the great Quill Gordon, Light Cahill, Greenwell's Glory, Gold-Ribbed Hare's Ear, plus many newer patterns.

Through experimentation by anglers and professional fly-tyers, the list is constantly lengthened. Among the relatively new and vastly popular wets are the Fledermaus, the Muddler Minnow streamers, and the woven-hair-bodied nymphs which are now being used extensively in the Rockies. And recent years have brought fame to such dry patterns as the Rat-Faced MacDougal, Gray Wulff (and other Wulff variations), Jassid, Irresistible, and a whole batch of small midges and terrestrial insects, such as beetles and ants. These little terrestrials, which originated with the "Pennsylvania school" of fly-tyers, have provided still further possibilities for dry-fly experimentation.

The name of the actual inventor of dry flies has been lost—if, indeed, one person was the inventor. Late in the nineteenth century a number of factors made the development of the dry fly almost inevitable. One was the introduction of the split-cane fly rod. Here was an instrument that could not only reach out to shy fish in clear, low water, but could also flick the droplets off a fly and dry it on the false cast. Then came the vacuum-dressed silk

A present-day fly collection showing the wide range of sunk flies: nymphs, emergers, wet flies, streamers and lures.

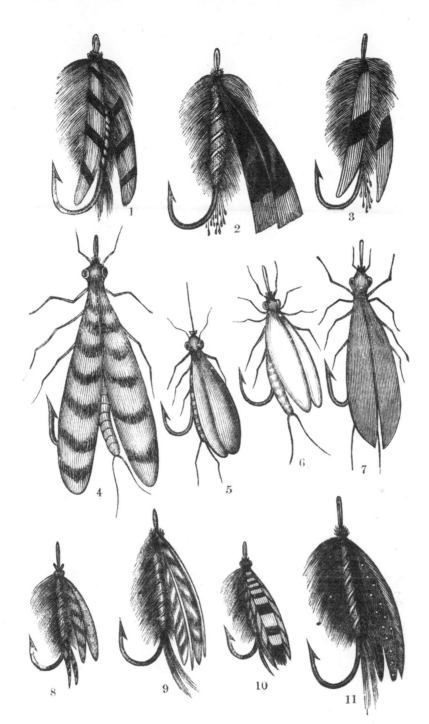

"Exact imitation" is hardly a new idea, as these artificial stone flies and caddis flies from the last century prove.

line that brought out the potential of the bamboo as the older braided horsehair and linen lines never could. And perhaps most important of all was Henry Sinclair Hall's perfection of the mass-produced, eyed trout hook. Before it appeared on the market in 1879, trout hooks were "blind." Their tapered shanks were whipped to a piece of gut or to a single strand of horsehair. Changing a sodden fly for a fresh one under those circumstances meant changing the leader, or at least part of it. Without the eyed hook, dry-fly fishing would have been too tedious to become popular. And it was with the rising popularity of the dry fly late in the last half of the nineteenth century that the hackle feather became the rightful center of fly-tying attention. For a dry fly must float on its hackle tips, and most of its effectiveness depends on hackle quality and color.

Halford and his crew of dry-fly zealots had little difficulty obtaining their feathers. Since their numbers were small, their demands were not large. As a matter of doctrine, they cast only to rising fish; this meant that even mediocre hackle could be used, because the fly had long periods of inactivity in which to dry off. Lastly, cock fighting had been abolished as recently as 1849, and many a stiff-hackled cock still strutted the British barnyards.

The dry fly was launched in America in 1885, when Halford sent a set of his dry flies to Theodore Gordon in New York State. Gordon was an inventive and observant sportsman. He realized that Halford's flies imitated British insects and that insects on this side of the Atlantic were quite different. He originated many impressionistic imitations of the naturals he found on his own favorite streams—the Quill Gordon being perhaps the most famous of his patterns. His flies seem a bit large-winged to us today, and the style of winging has changed slightly, but the present-day master tyers of the Catskills carry on his basic tradition.

The first American book on dry-fly fishing didn't appear until some twenty years after Gordon began his experiments, and by the time the dry fly became really popular here, a bit after World War I, the materials situation was becoming acute. First, American demands on hackle were far more severe than Britain's. Our streams are more turbulent than Halford's stately chalkstreams. Only the very stiffest hackle would do. Then, too, our insects are larger, and a bigger, heavier hook has to be supported. And, finally, casting only to the rise doesn't work well here. An angler must prospect likely water in our mountain streams, rise or no rise. So the fly must float, cast after cast, with only a false cast or two to dry it.

Even today, there is no synthetic dry-fly hackle on the market, nor any miracle chemical that can transform soft hackle into needle-sharp barbs. Superb hackle can float a fly unaided, but the pioneer dry-fly anglers in England often resorted to coating the hackle with paraffin solutions. Theodore Gordon frequently used kerosene. Until a few years ago, standard fly-line dressing was dissolved in gasoline or the less flammable carbon tet. Now we have the superior silicone preparations, which represent another advance in fly-fishing, but this is not to say the problem has been solved. Poor hackle still floats poorly.

By the time the dry fly gained wide acceptance in America, the source of hackle supply was diminishing. Not only had cock fighting long been outlawed here, but the agricultural revolution had transformed chicken-raising into a mass-production industry, to the detriment of the hackle supply. Birds were now bred for fast growth and plump breasts, or for greater egg production. Certainly not for first-class hackles. And to top it all off, most cockerels were killed for fryers when only months old.

To see the full implications of this fly-tyer's nightmare, you must understand a few facts about the nature of the bird that bears the indispensable hackle. All of our current breeds of chickens are descendants of a wild bird from India called the Bankiva fowl. The males of the species are extremely polygamous and, hence, highly combative. While the females have unimposing neck feathers, the males have long, stiff, glossy hackles, which protect the vulnerable neck and throat area from the leg spurs and beaks of rivals. Since the bird that survives the fight gets the hens and begets the chicks, birds with the stiffest neck feathers prospered. The process of natural selection toward stiff neck feathers was started in the wild and continued until cock fighting was outlawed. Then the purveyors of eggs and white meat stepped in, and the tyer had to scout the ever-decreasing subsistence farms for a source of supply.

How then, you may ask, is the current army of several million flyfishermen supplied? The answer is, poorly — except for the anglers who deal with top custom tyers. General stores, hardware stores, and even sports shops have to take what they can get.

Most of the hackle is soft, and half of it has been dyed — a process that further reduces the quality of already indifferent hackle. The necks are bought in bulk from importers who buy them by the hundreds of thousands in India. Most of these necks are ginger, red, or white—useful colors, but not the full spectrum a tyer would like. A few of the necks are first-rate, and you're fortunate if you can pick and choose from a boxful. But commercial houses can't afford such sorting and discarding. Surprisingly, top-notch flies can still be obtained if you know the right professional tyer. There are a few of these men left, yet very few young tyers are coming up. The reason is that there's no money in producing quality flies.

A tyer must raise most of his own roosters. True, some necks in the more common colors can be picked up from a friendly importer, but none is likely to be found in the all-important shades called natural duns. These are a slaty blue-grey color, and fly-tyers have made their reputations on their dun hackles. To get such hackles, birds must be bred, crossbred, pampered, and plucked, and the price of doing this is almost confiscatory. Yet nearly half of the most popular dry flies call for this shade, and a dyed feather always shows a bogus blue or purplish tinge when held up to the light—which is precisely how a trout sees it.

To get the natural duns, you have to raise a lot of birds. About fifty percent of the eggs hatched will produce cocks, but only a few of them will have top-quality hackle. Then, too, the blue-dun color is recessive. No matter how you breed, you'll end up with lots of badger (white with black center), black, and white hackles. Only a small percentage will be true duns.

Since I myself have raised birds for hackles, I can readily understand the economic plight of the professional tyer. It cost me $10 a year per rooster just for the special small-grain feed that hackle-producing birds are supposed to have. It takes two years for birds to reach full maturity, so a bird has eaten $20 worth of feed before he starts producing.

With luck, a bird should produce excellent hackle for several years. A prize rooster is seldom killed; he is plucked with tender, loving care three or four times a year.

Curiously, despite the costs and risks of trying to raise excellent hackle, flies tied with these superior materials by the finest artists of the day cost only pennies more than run-of-the-mill shop-tied flies. I once asked Walt Dette, the master fly-tyer of Roscoe, New York, why this should be so. "It's all the traffic will bear," he explained. "After all, trout flies are expendable. The average guy leaves several of them in trees during a day's fishing. Who'd pay a buck for a fly?"

There is only one factor that sweetens the pot for independent, custom tyers. There's no middleman. The feathers go straight from rooster to fisherman, and fly-tyer takes all. Even so, most fly-tyers drive old cars. And the finest craftsman that I ever knew gave it all up to work in a barbershop a few years back. Once a man has paid for the hooks, thread, wax, and other purchasable materials — not to mention costs of rooster-raising — he can't tie much more than $8 or $10 worth of flies in an hour. If machines

Wild jungle fowl rooster and subservient mate as seen in Asia. This strain is disappearing—and so is our best hackle.

were available, the economic picture might be brighter. But every fly must be tied from start to finish by hand.

What, then, keeps the few remaining perfectionists in the business? Pride, certainly. The good life, probably, too. Tyers live near good fishing and shooting. But there seems to be more to it than that. They are celebrities in the eyes of dedicated fishermen. Their advice is sought by presidents and board chairmen. You stand in line to get their flies and you don't dare annoy them even if your order doesn't arrive by opening day.

Since the basic materials of most flies have always come from the barnyard, it's natural that there's a touch of barnyard earthiness in some of the flies themselves. One all-time favorite is named the Cow Dung because it imitates a green-bodied fly that is usually found on meadow muffins. Another classic is the Tup's Indispensable, invented by R. S. Austin of Tiverton in Devon. The exact dressing of this killing fly was a closely kept secret for years. Sound business was one reason. Victorian prudery another. For how would you explain to a nineteenth-century gentlewoman that the beautifully translucent yellow body was dubbed with urine-stained hair taken from the indispensable portion of a ram, or tup?

The famous Hendrickson dry fly originated by Roy Steenrod, an early pupil of Theodore Gordon's, has a similar origin. The body is dubbed with fur from the crotch of a red fox vixen, which has a permanent pink stain.

Those are some of the more esoteric materials—including a few of the most expensive ones. Feathers, and particularly hackles, are still pivotal to fly-tying and to fly-fishing, but long evenings at the tying vice produce a lot of experimentation. In streamer flies, maribou stork feathers with their octopus-like action are rivaling bucktail and saddle hackles. Silk floss and similar body materials have always had their place, but newer materials are now finding other uses. For instance, tarnish-proof strips of Mylar tinsel are showing up more and more in the wings of these flies.

Bucktail flies obviously get their name from the deer tail of which they're made, and this material has always been plentiful. Because of its texture, consistency, and length, it is valuable for many wet-fly effects. In a way, its versatility makes it more valuable than that special hair from a vixen. The deer hair that's being displaced nowadays in streamers is popping up in, of all places, dry-fly dressing. Many of the shaggy but effective Wulff flies have bucktail tails and wings. Harry Darbee's inspired Rat-Faced MacDougal and the series of variations that have followed it sport bodies of clipped deer hair.

These flies may be a bit chunky for delicate mayfly imitations, but they are the only flies that will float in a downpour. And since a pelting rain can knock enough insects out of the bushes to make a pool boil, such flies represent another deadly set of lures.

In wet flies, fluorescent flosses are also appearing these days—particularly in the bodies of salmon flies. They give off a glow on dark days or in the depths, causing many anglers to swear by them. Synthetics aren't really new; J. W. Dunne of England popularized them back in the Twenties. In *Sunshine and the Dry-Fly*, he advocated a series of artificials with bodies of cellulite floss over white-painted hook shanks. When annointed with oil, these bodies had a succulent translucency. They haven't been on the market since World War II, but new types of brightly glowing synthetics are being tied into wet patterns.

These changes in materials and in flies tell a lot about trends in fishing. Most of Halford's original split-wing floaters were winged with dun-colored starling primary feathers and epitomized the ultrarealistic approach. Theodore Gordon leaned toward bunched wood-duck flank feathers glimpsed through the hackle. He was an impressionist. Darbee's Rat-Faced and the Wulff flies are highly utilitarian and offer a good mouthful. Experimenting with shapes can probably go just so far, but experimenting with materials, from the dullest to the most garishly fluorescent, will probably never end.

Happily, the materials used for wet flies, nymphs, and streamers, whether new or old in dressing style, remain in good supply. A Royal Coachman, for instance, utilizes golden-pheasant tippet, peacock herl, red silk floss, red-brown cock or hen hackle, and white primary goose or duck quill. A fly-tyer has little trouble obtaining these items.

Salmon-fly materials felt the pinch early in this century when many feathers were proscribed by international treaties. Indian crow, cock of the rock, toucan, and bustard disappeared from the salmon-fly repertory, but suitable and effective substitutes have been found, and the fully dressed fly of today is hard to distinguish from its nineteenth-century prototype (though smaller, less fully dressed salmon flies have also gained wide acceptance).

Fortunately, the banned feathers were used mainly as color accents. The most widely used exotics—golden pheasant, English jay, summer duck, florican, European kingfisher, blue-and-yellow and red-and-yellow macaw, silver pheasant, and the rest—are still available to fly-tyers even though they can be quite expensive.

The demand for these materials is not increasing, because salmon-fishing tactics have changed considerably. In the good old days, it was mainly an early spring and late fall sport. Salmon were considered uncatchable in low water and warm weather. The British now use smaller, less colorful, more sparsely dressed flies during the summer and have opened up a whole new season for the sport. And in Canada the fishing is mostly from late June through September, and the same small, relatively drab flies are now most popular there, too.

Most of these flies are winged with hair or with the natural plumage of various ducks like widgeon, teal, and mallard. Usually such feathers are relatively easy to obtain from hunting friends, but bulk shipments from overseas are under continuous attack by the National Audubon Society. While the Society's main objection is to the use of the feathers by the millinery trade, tyers feel threatened, too.

The Audubon people are worthy opponents. A few years ago an Audubon friend of mine told me with some satisfaction that a member of his chapter was head inspector of feathers for the New York customs department. "You fly-tyers can't fool him," he claimed. "Why, he can tell what kind of bird almost any feather comes from, and you can bet he catches lots of contraband shipments." I had the last word, though. I told him that a fifth-generation salmon-fly tyer I knew who came from Ireland could do that dead drunk. And, when sober, this man could tell which square inch of the bird the feather came from and estimate the bird's age accurately! He really could, too.

Of course, these economic and legal tugs of war that plague the fly-tyer are little noticed by the world at large. Only once, to my knowledge, did fly-tying hit the headlines. Late in the last century, a man was killed in northern Ireland following a heated discussion about the precise shade of dyed seal's fur that should be used in dubbing the body of Michael Rogan's Fiery Brown salmon fly. However, one has to suspect that some fiery brown liquid may have been more to blame for this crime of passion than the fly itself.

When fly-tyers and flyfishermen do make news, it is generally conservation news which appears in publications devoted to the subject or is, unfortunately, relegated to the back pages of the papers. For these men are extremely active in conservation groups that fight pollution, wanton industrial development of wild areas, and similar threats to wildlife. And even though flies are so deadly in expert hands that they may, as Hewitt stated, take every trout in a stream, the flyfisherman is the trout's best friend. He may catch ninety percent of the trout that are netted on our hard-fished streams, but he understands that running water will support only so many fish, and he knows of the scarcity of running water itself. He releases most of the fish he catches, to avoid depleting a limited population.

His sport allows him to do so, and this is another angling advance that is virtually unique to the fly. A fly-caught fish is almost always lip-hooked and easy to release. Treble-hook plugs and spoons and bait hooks which are easily swallowed are another matter. Studies have shown that nearly half of all worm-hooked, undersized trout soon die. The comparative figure for fly-hooked fish is three percent, and this estimate is not restricted just to barbless flies; the figure would be much lower for the many flyfishermen who carefully remove the barbs from their hooks.

So, even though the lure may be deadly, the man may be merciful. And there's wisdom in this. It's better to enjoy golden eggs than to eat goose.

# The Curious Case
# of the Caddis

"The little log cabin that walks" seems to fascinate young children more than any other common animal. I think it was the first of nature's great mysteries pointed out to me when I was very young, and I was astounded when I discovered there was a "bug" inside the bundle of twigs. I also remember being told this crawling creature was a caddis, but that was about the sum total of my knowledge about these insects until I'd waded well into my trout-fishing adulthood.

Surprisingly, most fishermen I talk to today know little more than that, and yet, if mayflies may make up the butter in trout diets, caddis flies are certainly their daily bread. Many of the larval forms — especially the log cabin that walks and similar species—are readily available to trout, day and night, winter and summer, as they crawl slowly over the rocks without cover or camouflage. Mayfly nymphs, on the other hand, are more a feast-or-famine proposition, for most of them hide under rocks or debris or burrow in the sand during the greater part of their lives until they have to expose themselves in hatching.

In early spring, especially, the trout's dependence on caddis larvae has become part of our folklore. An old-time Yankee mountain-brook fisherman once gave me the word on trout behavior while he was cleaning his mess of opening-day brookies.

"See all that sand and gravel in the gut? That's ballast. Keeps him from being washed downstream in this high water. That's why you got to get down to them in April. You can't put on too many split shot. Their bellies got them anchored to the bottom."

The man's remedy may have been right, but his diagnosis was all wrong. Trout aren't smart enough—or dumb enough—to eat pebbles and gravel. They don't need it for their crops as wildfowl do, and they have no use for that much roughage to keep regular. You find such stuff in trout stomachs along with pine needles and small twigs only because that's what the meal of the day comes packaged in. And the cased caddis larva is by far the most readily available form of insect food in nearly all our running waters.

Mayflies may be the foundation of our fly-fishing practices, but the much-neglected caddis flies play at least as important a part in the trout's scheme of things. On many acid Eastern streams they far outnumber the mayflies. On the limestone streams of eastern Pennsylvania and in some mineral-rich waters of the West the balance may tip the other way, but the caddis never come out worse than a close second to the mayflies and are far more important than the stone flies and the true flies put together.

Even the number of separate species seems to rival the range of the mayflies. In the British Isles alone some 189 species of caddis have been identified. And here in North America, where we have many more disparate ecological regions, the count is far higher: 568. This tally was made back in the Thirties, but the dean of caddis collectors, when he added them up at that time, admitted that his own research—and the work of others he quoted—had all been done before 1910 and they had probably only scratched the surface. It seems reasonable to suppose that we have nearly a thousand species here, though we won't know for certain until the taxonomists pay more attention to the order of Trichoptera. And that, in case you want to dazzle your friends, is the official Latin name, meaning hairy-winged, for the entire order of caddis flies. But there are far more useful things fishermen should know about them.

Caddis flies are close relatives of the moths. Both orders of insects have pronounced antennae and both have wings covered with small scales; they advance through similar life-stages, they look much alike in their adult forms, and they're both attracted to bright lights at night. Moths, however, are usually heavier in the body, their antennae are fancier, they tend to fold their wings in a horizontal plane rather than in the inverted "V" of the caddis, and, of course, they spend their formative days on land instead of under water.

In the beginning, all caddis flies are minute eggs which quickly separate from one another after they've been deposited as a cluster by the mated female. At this stage in life, and at this stage alone, the insect is probably safe from the hungry trout. The speck-like eggs are far too small to be picked off the bottom if the fish notice them.

Once they have hatched out and started to grow as worm-like larvae, caddis are eaten by trout at every opportunity. Caddis, for some reason, appear to be especially delicious. I have seen some stone flies that are carefully avoided by trout and I know of some mayflies that the trout feed on only occasionally and indifferently, but I have yet to see a caddis that wasn't gobbled with relish. Caddis are so tasty and nutritious that trout are not deterred by the abrasive houses of sticks and stones most species stick together with a silklike secretion, though these protective casings may help fend off smaller minnows and carnivorous stone flies.

During this longest stage of their lives, caddis show a great diversity in color, size and lifestyle. Most species are vegetarians, feeding on live algae or on dead forms of larger vegetable matter such as leaves and blades of sedge grass, but a few are definitely carnivorous, preying on fellow caddis and on other aquatic insects. Some types manage without the protection of the "cabin," or turtle-like carapace, never building any cases at all for themselves. They live under rocks or in crannies, and a few of these highly specialized varieties spin small, spider-like nets to strain food out of the passing current.

All these types of caddis larvae are undoubtedly eaten by trout, but the case-builders, the ones that lead relatively exposed lives, probably contribute most heavily to the trout's diet. Fishermen have been imitating these cases for years, yet the artificials have never been very popular. One of the earliest and most famous is the long, bristly "Strawman" which is tied out of deer hair and is a good general replica of many large, case-building caddis species.

The problem with case-builder imitations is that they are

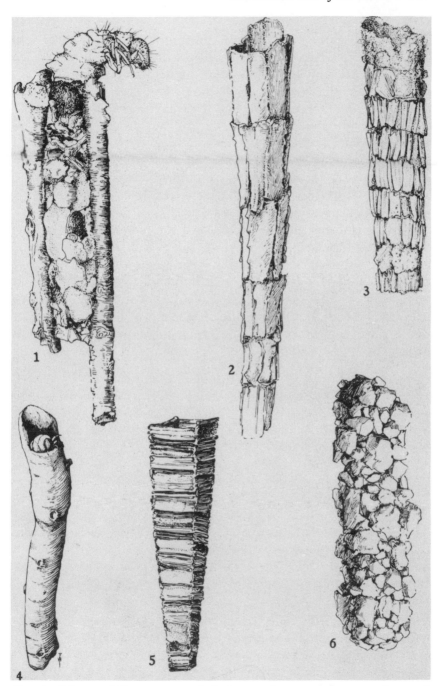

Case-building caddis construct their houses in many shapes and out of many materials. The prevalent shad fly lives in #5.

difficult to present realistically in flowing water. It may be easy to drag them slowly along the bottom with a sinking line when fishing ponds and lakes, but how can you mimic this bottom-creeping behavior in a river when the current keeps hurrying your line and leader downstream? And when the river is high and roily — the very time when caddis are drifting down-current in an easy-to-imitate manner — the less-abrasive large stone flies and mayflies are being dislodged, too, and most anglers prefer to fish with the popular artificials of these suddenly available nymphs.

The caddis larva itself, when removed from its case, has a strong enough appeal to trout so that it is a highly popular live bait all over Europe. The great American naturalist, John Burroughs, used the stick-caddis worm as live bait for brook trout as his first choice whenever fly-fishing became unproductive—or so a friend who knew and fished with him once told me. Why trout have such a hearty appetite for the naked worm they never see without its clothes on baffles me. A while ago the outdoor writer Raleigh Boaze sent me some beautiful imitations of large caddis worms tied with semitranslucent latex bodies. They're extremely effective, another proof of the trout's phenomenal if puzzling appetite for the caddis.

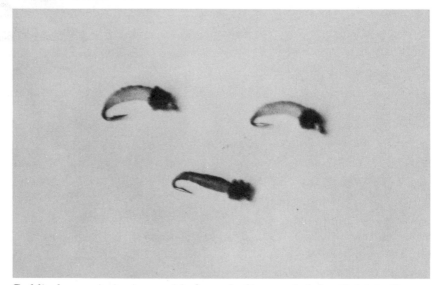

Caddis larvae imitations with latex bodies as tied by Raleigh Boaze. Trout never see them this naked—yet they work.

Once the larva is fully grown, which usually takes a year, it anchors its case firmly to a rock with silk threads and covers up the open end of its house. At this stage it becomes semidormant, taking no food for a week or two. It has now entered the semifinal, or pupal, form and is starting to look a little more like the winged insect it will become. If you pull the animal out of its case at this point, you will see its embryonic wings drooping small and dark along its sides and the long adult antennae wrapped elaborately around its body. In this walled-up, motionless state, the caddis is less tempting to the trout (and is difficult for the angler to imitate) but this armistice doesn't last long.

When the pupating caddis is finally ready to advance to its final stage in life it must run the gauntlet again. It then chews off the cover of its case and shoots rapidly to the surface, propelled by its long, oar-like middle legs and given a further upward assist by a bubble of gas that's forming between the pupal skin and the rapidly developing adult, winged insect inside.

This combination of buoyancy and swimming proficiency makes the emerging caddis a difficult target for even the nimblest trout. In fact, because fish miss so many at this time, one of the surest signs that trout are feeding on caddis instead of the more easily captured mayfly is the sight of an insect zigzagging upward from a boil on the surface. An emerging caddis is tantalizing, and trout can't resist chasing it, even though it's one of the few insect foods they miss with great regularity.

If the trout are having trouble with the caddis at this stage, the fisherman is in an even worse predicament. How can he make his sunk imitation perform like a small rocket taking off for the surface? The only way I've found to duplicate this is to wade directly up-current of feeding fish, stop the cast so that the line falls in a series of loose curves in front of me, and wait till the current pulls the line straight. If I've estimated the distance to the trout's lie accurately, the fly, which has been sinking on the slack line, will start for the surface when the line pulls tight. This is an exacting presentation, however, that calls for perilous wading, and you put down a lot of good fish stumbling down the middle of the current trying to execute it.

And this is only the beginning of your problems. What should your imitation look like? Even if you're familiar with the species of caddis that's hatching out, having studied both the pupae and the winged adults, which form should your artificial favor? How rapidly is the fly developing as it shoots up toward the surface? How does its color appear to the fish when viewed through the gas bubble that lies between the gray, chitinous skin and the living insect inside? These are questions that few anglers can answer. I've never met anyone who's actually observed an emerging pupa making its explosive trip to the surface, and I've talked to many dedicated anglers who've raised larvae in their aquaria in the hope of just such a sighting.

Imitation of this stage in the insect's life, and of its mercurial behavior pattern, is the least explored frontier of fly-fishing and perhaps the most promising one. I have been experimenting for several years with imitations of a few of the more common species and I have to admit I've had no great successes to date. I have had best results with gray- or gray-brown-bodied imitations, though I hesitate to give this as a general prescription. I know one caddis species that has a bright green body as a pupa but acquires a brassy dun color a few seconds later as a mature adult. I've had good fishing with both colors at different times during this hatch, but neither one works well all the time and I sometimes wonder if it isn't the presentation rather than the imitation itself that's responsible. I'm afraid I'll have to bring you more problems than solutions at this time, but I know several expert flyfishermen who are working in this area and perhaps there will soon be a pool of knowledge available on emerging caddis.

Although the most important species of caddis I'm acquainted with seem to emerge in this manner, not all the many species do. I know of at least one early-season caddis that crawls out on rocks or logs to hatch the way most stone flies do. And I have every belief that some types hatch under water, as the Quill Gordon mayfly does, making the trip to the surface as mature, winged insects. There seems to be no pat solution to imitating emergers, and perhaps that's a blessing. Fishing might not be so much fun if we knew all the answers.

Many emerging caddis probably never make it to the air, even though they temporarily escape the trout. As we have all observed in the case of hatching mayflies, a considerable proportion are malformed or damaged in the act of emerging from their nymphal

Imitation of the emerging caddis pupa with low-slung, short wings. Is this the way they look to trout under the surface?

cases, and these unfortunates drift downstream till they are eaten or drowned in a rapids. Then, too, since weaker specimens of the smaller species probably have difficulty in fighting their way through the rubbery film of surface tension, many must drown at the edge of success. Perhaps for this reason, a great addition to our fly boxes during caddis hatches would be accurate imitations of adult insects patterned on the old wet fly which could be fished dead drift.

We must suppose, however, that at least a majority of the pupae hatch successfully and present the fisherman with another challenge. Some specimens seem to shoot out of the water, fully fledged like a Poseidon missile, while others don't make such a clean getaway. They buzz and flutter on the surface erratically for a moment or two before they become airborne. To a trout that has probably recently missed an emerger right at the surface, this is too much to resist. And this is where presentation of the adult, winged imitations takes over. But before we look into imitations and the methods of presenting them, it's important to realize that there are other times, too, when trout will be looking for and feeding on adult caddis flies. Once they've hatched, these flies don't die in a day or so the way mayflies do. Adults of some species seem to take nourishment or at least water during their winged state and live for several weeks in this form instead of the day or so allotted to the mayflies. This is important, for the caddis that have hatched out on previous days will probably return in flights to the river in the evening whether or not this is the night when their mating and egg-laying will take place. Admittedly, many of them remain several feet above the water on the upstream flight, but a significant number also fly just off the surface and occasionally touch the water. Can you imagine anything more exciting to trout than a cloud of flies easily visible overhead? When a fly does make a mistake and come within reach, the rise is usually explosive.

Then, of course, there are the mated adults that have finished with their nightly water-play and are nearing the end of their lives. Many of the males probably fall dead or dying on the surface, while the females buzz, hop, or skitter on the surface in the act of egg-laying. Again the trout feast on easily available adults. Why most fishermen have neglected dry imitations of the various caddis species over the years baffles me. Trout look for these flies, rise to them, then look for more. And the major caddis hatches last longer than mayfly hatches. The emergers, water-players, and egg-layers of some species appear on or over the water night after night for more than a month.

The dry fly at these times is the logical choice and yet very little attention has been paid to floating caddis imitations. Frederick M. Halford, who launched the dry fly in Britain nearly 100 years ago, included five caddis patterns in his final selection of 33 dry flies recommended for the chalkstreams of southern England. But when his flies and theories crossed the Atlantic a few years later, only the mayfly imitations seemed to survive the passage.

Fortunately, caddis imitations of sorts did spring up in several regional forms here in America, but most were far less accurate and effective than Halford's original quill-winged replicas. All-hackle flies, including bivisibles and variants were, perhaps, intended to be loose imitations of caddis with their wings aflutter. The Adams from Michigan is said to represent a caddis, but, though it's one of the few great all-purpose flies, its outline looks much more like a mayfly to me. It is from the free-wheeling West rather than from the effete East that our best early caddis imitations came. I've recently seen high-floating patterns with downwings of elk or deer hair which appear to be true regional innovations that have been used in the Rockies and the Far West for years. As impressionistic artificials for fast-water fishing they are hard to fault, except, perhaps, for the limited color-range.

No matter how realistic the artificial, however, it can't do the whole job by itself. The caddis silhouette is certainly unique and needs accurate duplication to deceive the trout, but the *behavior* of the insect on the surface is equally distinctive, and classic dry-fly presentation makes no accommodation to this fact. Caddis flies are far more active than mayflies are, and the purist's dead-drift approach doesn't seem to telegraph the caddis message to the trout.

Caddis hop, flutter, and bounce on the surface. Duplicating this behavior with a dropper fly danced on the surface was easy for our great-grandparents with their 10-foot-plus rods and light lines, but you can't begin to do this job with the stubby sticks that modern flyfishers use. The most likely tactic with modern tackle is to cast to a fish across and downstream and give the fly a little "nudge" just before it passes over the fish's lie. This "sudden

The most popular caddis imitation in past years has been the killing Adams. Tail and wings seem mayflyish to me.

inch" will more than double your rises when fishing a caddis imitation if—and this is an all-important *if*—this staccato minimotion is in an *upstream* direction. Caddis always fly upstream, whether they're hatching out, returning for the fun of it, or egg-laying, so any motion in any other direction shouts "fake" to the trout.

I realize that moving a dry fly in any way or in any direction is in strict violation of the classic dry-fly code laid down by Frederick M. Halford. I was given a vivid reminder of this fact a few years ago. Shortly after publication of my book, *Fishing the Dry Fly as a Living Insect*, I ran across Sparse Grey Hackle at a famous fly-tying-materials emporium. Sparse, in case you've never met him in person or through his books, is so universally acknowledged as the dean of fly-fishing writers that it is rumored he has connections with our patron, St. Peter. He is very definitely a man to be listened to. Sparse, on this occasion, walked up and said, "Congratulations, Len. I hear you've just written an entire book devoted to the ancient art of trolling." He is the kindest as well as the wittiest of men and there was a twinkle behind those bottle-cap glasses he wears. Nevertheless, I got the message loud and clear. I have not given up my sinful ways, though. I still twitch my caddis imitations and sometimes even my floating mayflies.

Since the caddis dry fly is best fished with vigor, it obviously must be tied in a style that floats extremely well. Variants and bivisibles fit the bill, but their silhouettes aren't realistic enough to fool many trout in slow or even streamy water. Bodies of clipped deer hair or cork aren't the answer even though they float well. Both types lie low in the water and leave a sizable wake in the surface film when moved — a behavior pattern that in no way resembles the tip-toeing caddis adult. The most effective fly I've found is built with stiff fiber wings—either of top quality spade hackles or of high-floating guard hairs of aquatic animals like the mink. This type of wing may sound a lot like the wing of the Western elk-hair caddis but, fortunately, I'd never seen those imitations when I started work on my designs or I'd probably have adopted the existing pattern and perpetuated their two shortcomings.

The first problem with elk or deer hair is that it greatly limits your choice of colors, while hackle and mink tail can be obtained, undyed, in almost any shade the tyer wants. More important, these fibers will lie absolutely straight and flat when tied in, whereas elk and deer hair, being hollow, will splay when pinched by the tying silk. This upward and outward flaring doesn't affect floating quality but it does alter the silhouette significantly. Next time a caddis lands on the outside of your window-pane at night examine it closely. What you'll be seeing is the "fish-eye view" from directly below—precisely what the trout sees when a caddis floats overhead. I think you'll be surprised at how trim and slim a caddis appears from this viewpoint when its wings are folded.

I named my patterns the *Fluttering Caddises* (because they should be fished with a slight motion, as if they were fluttering) and they are now advertised in the catalogs of several large suppliers and are obtainable at some retail tackle stores. Although most orders, I'm told, have come from Easterners, friends of mine who have experimented with these patterns out West say they're every bit as effective on the fast-water streams out there.

So, whether you consider them welcome friends or poor relatives, the caddises are very much with us. And as some authorities

The fluttering caddis gives up a point or two on exact imitation, but gains them back in mobility and floatability.

have pointed out, they're likely to increase in importance because they're a hardy tribe and aren't decimated by floods, marginal pollution, and stream erosion as are the more delicate mayflies.

Caddis flies differ from mayflies in many ways—in their life-cycle, in their longer seasonal availability to trout, and in their habits and appearance as adults. In their first several months of life they're important as trout food but a difficult proposition for flyfishers to duplicate in running water. During those split seconds when they're zooming toward the surface to hatch, they present problems both to the trout and to the angler who would imitate them. But once they hatch out, they're on or just above the surface for portions of many days—not just hours—or 10 to 20 times as long as mayflies are. Isn't this just what the dry-fly fisherman ordered?

# 15

## *Take Your Pick*

Fly-fishing wouldn't be half the game it is without the alibi, the reason why not. The big one may have got away (he almost always does), he may have refused — definitely — our most choice offerings, but that is never the end of it. The angler takes defeat hard. When forced to admit that he has indeed lost at Armageddon, he rises to the occasion—with an explanation. Drag. The leader — too long or too short, too heavy or too light. The fish — highly intelligent. But we overlook perhaps the best — and most valid — excuse: the fly itself. I know I did, until that morning on Colorado's Gunnison River.

It was a beautiful June day, and this was my first trip after four wartime, fishless years. The hatch was on, the fish were rising, and I was working a long, gliding pool that looked as if it should produce something extra special in the way of trout. I tied on a #12 Ginger Quill and proceeded confidently to the business at hand. Five casts and no fish later, it was apparent that something was wrong. Puzzled, I picked an insect out of the eddy behind my waders and checked it against my imitation. In size and color it was a close double. Must be drag, I thought, and started casting a wavy line. It was five minutes before I got any attention. A fish came up under the fly, followed it back, and dropped down again. But he had taken a good close look at my fly, and, for the first time, so had I.

What was it doing? Well, it was riding tail down, eye pointing skyward. I tried another fly. This one was better. A fish even nosed it once. But it had flaws. On almost every cast it lay flat on its side, wings touching the water, a far cry from the tiptoe-prancing naturals that were coasting down from the riffle. And so it went. I got some good fish, but it wasn't a star performance.

Since that long-ago trip I've examined thousands of flies and worked out a set of standards for the ones I use. The average trout-fisher, who doesn't tie his own flies and who therefore probably doesn't scrutinize each imitation very carefully, may find these criteria helpful. Remember: All flies are *not* created equal—not even those tied by the same man and displayed in the same compartment on the tackle-store counter. And this is just as true of flies you've tied yourself, by the way. Some will definitely be better than others. How do you pick out those that are most likely to succeed?

A good dry fly is a thing of beauty and a joy on the stream. But it's easier to get a dud in this category than in any other. Little things are magnified when it comes to floaters. Only the very best cock properly. The first thing to check is the wings. Are they the same length? The same width? Are they unsplit? Turn the fly so

*Left:* a good dry fly. *Right:* all the mistakes—skimpy tail, uneven body, short, scraggly hackle, and uneven wings.

that you're looking it straight in the eye, which, by the way, must be closed properly. It can cut a leader or slip off if it isn't. From this angle, the wings should be just two curved lines. If one or both are slanted off to the sides, the fly will behave like a propeller — and that's bad.

Are the wings directly on top of the hook? I don't mean they shouldn't form a V — and how wide a V is purely a matter of taste — but if you extend the line formed by the bend of the hook to the top side of the hook, it should bisect the angle made by the two wings. If it doesn't, the fly will probably ride off-kilter.

Now take a look at the hackle. It's pretty hard to judge the quality of hackle without a lot of experience. Chances are all flies in the same box were hackled from the same rooster anyway, so don't worry much about hackle stiffness unless you're shopping from store to store. Some flies may be more heavily hackled than others, though. I pick bushier hackles for fast water and sparse ones for slower streams. Beware of the short-hackled fly. Sometimes the tips of the hackle extend no farther from the shank of the hook than the point does. Try to pick out flies that have a hackle length that measures from 1½ to 1¾ the width of the hook gape. Flies that are too short in the hackle have the habit of lying on their sides.

Moving back toward the tail of the fly, give the body a casual check, even though this part is the least likely to fail. If it's made of quill or fur, it should be wound smoothly, without bumps or bare spots. Sharp trout teeth can catch on bumps and bare spots and start unraveling the body.

Now to the tail itself, a prime danger spot. A defect there can cause a lot of woe. Flies from the same lot may show a great resemblance in tail length and tail bushiness, but if you look closely, you'll find a certain amount of variation. Pick the longest and the bushiest — within reason, of course. It's hard to overdo on this point; for every fly that lands on its head (too much tail), there are ten that land tail down. One final check. Drop the fly on the counter from the height of a foot or so. If it lands just the way you'd like to see it on the water, you're in. Even if it doesn't, the odds are pretty good if it answers in all other respects.

Follow the same general procedure for other types of dry fly. With hairwings, like the Wulff flies and the Irresistibles, your

Splayed tail fibers of this dry fly (seen on water surface) add to floatability and proper cocking without bulk.

special interest should be concentrated on the wings; after all, they're at least twice as big. If they aren't perfect, you're in for it! Be sure that the hair bunches are closely matched in amount of fiber and in length. I always avoid the flies with the longest wings, no matter how perfectly matched they may be. Too much wing can make the fly top-heavy, so that it rolls on its side after hitting the water.

Watch the tail section on variants and spiders. With all that long hackle up front, it stands to reason they need a longer and thicker tail than usual to make a perfect two-point landing. Bivisibles seem to be the easiest to pick out, the hardest to miss on. No matter how they're tied, they seem to float perfectly. I like them evenly hackled, though, and tapered toward the tail.

One last point on this category. Nothing, not even a woman's mind, is changed as often as a man's dry fly. It makes sense to choose one with some shank showing between the hook eye and the winding. This space will make it easier to pick off that little piece of leader left when you snip off a fly and prevent it from unwinding at the head.

Any fly will sink, after a fashion, but that doesn't mean you shouldn't be careful when you choose a wet fly, though I grant you an error here isn't nearly so fatal. Check the eye of the hook for perfect closure. Look for smooth heads, well lacquered against inadvertent unwinding. Inspect the body carefully. You can pretty nearly disregard the size and shape of the tail, though. As long as it's there it will do the job. Wings aren't crucial either, but they should be evenly matched and dead-centered for better swim. Don't short-change yourself on tinsel. Pick the shiniest; it's put there to glitter.

Hackle problems are few and far between on sunken flies. Do choose sparse flies, though. (After all, an insect has only six legs.) They sink better and they ride better in the current. I learned this fundamental a few years back on New York's Beaverkill River. My bushy March Brown wet looked plenty buggy to me, and the fish seemed to agree. They kept hitting it, anyway. Trouble was, I wasn't hooking many. A check of the hook point proved that sharpness had nothing to do with failure. Frustrating hours later I hit on the culprit—the fly. It was riding flat on its side. When I slacked off, it sank, hook down, as it should. But when I pulled on it, the fly went over on its side.

A poor wet fly: lumpy body, hackle too long, wings oversized and so uneven that fly will not swim properly through water.

Good wet-fly design: even, low-lying wings, sparse hackle, and slim body promise good entry and good travel in current.

I began pruning with a vengeance. The next time that fly hit water it had only a few wisps below the shank, and the point of the hook keeled it perfectly even in the swift current. I started to fill the creel then, and every fish was hooked firmly in the lower jaw.

The same reasoning should be applied to nymph selection. The sparser the hackle the better. Be sure also to check the eye of the hook and the head and to look for smooth, even bodies — unless it's one of those shaggy beasts.

With streamers and bucktails I go for the sparser models, too, mainly because they sink quicker. Otherwise I simply check the head and eye. If the body is tinseled, I go for the biggest shine. It's not a bad idea to look over the feathers or hair; they should be centered on top. If they're too far off, a streamer won't keel well either.

It's hard to go wrong on a big bass fly. They're usually tied on such heavy hooks that they ride perfectly, no matter how bushy. Besides, they're retrieved a lot slower and in much slower current. Again, head, eye, and body are the key places to inspect.

I don't know whether deer-hair bass and trout bugs should be classified as flies or not, but here are a few pointers, anyway. Be on the lookout for bald spots when you check the bodies. They'll float better and they'll be less likely to shed and unravel if they're uniform. And by all means pick the ones that are clipped closest to the hook shank on the underside, added insurance that they'll land right side up every time. More important, it gives clearance to the hook point, which means more fish per strike.

So much for the rules. Let's go one step further. Check on your judgment when you get to the stream. Suppose you are working with wet flies, streamers, and nymphs. When you tie on a new one, dangle it in the current close to you and see how it rides. Twitch it and see if it starts to flip over on its side. Now's the time to adjust with minor surgery, not after missing the best fish of the day. If you're a dry-fly man you can save hours of fruitless casting if you follow this one rule. Every time you put on a new fly, cast it straight upstream on a slack line and watch it carefully as it floats past you. Give it a few trials. If it's a chronic misbehaver, take it off and try another.

Remember, the perfect fly has probably never been tied. If it has, it was an accident. But most flies will work and work well. The idea is to choose the best from the better. Theodore Gordon, the father of American dry-fly fishing, advised the angler to "cast your flies with confidence." That's a lot easier to do when you know you've really *picked* them.

# The Blue-Nosed Fly

Today it seems hard to believe that barely sixty years ago the English-speaking world was reveling in the strictest sporting code that man has ever imposed upon himself. Yet well within the memories of men still actively fishing in these days of as-you-like-it morals and will-o'-the-wisp values, the loftiest and most rigid sportsman's dogma of all time — the dry-fly purist ethic — held sway in America, in Britain, and in Britain's then-vast colonies.

So passionately were these rules of sporting honor upheld by Victorian and Edwardian gentlemen that breaking them was as unthinkable as striking a woman in public. A transgressor could expect to be called a blackguard, sent to Coventry, or even asked to resign from his club.

There had been rules governing sport for centuries, of course, but these were easy to understand and explain. They had evolved gradually from the code of chivalry which had swept out of southern France during the Middle Ages and had exerted a wide influence on all rituals and behavior. Since sports in those days were essentially war games for aristocrats, many forms of the chase had adopted the protocols that knights considered proper in combat.

In falconry, for example, there was as distinct a pecking order governing the ownership of birds as there was for position on the battlefield. The large and rare gyrfalcon was reserved for emperors and the like, while lesser nobility had to be content with lesser birds. Overstepping your bird-rank in those days promised even sterner social penalties than those meted out to today's junior executive who drives a Rolls-Royce up to the country club and parks it beside his president's Buick.

By the early nineteenth century, however, ancient war sports like falconry and chasing the stag on horseback had nearly died out, and war itself had become less chivalrous as shrapnel replaced the sabre. The knight's code did not die with him, though. It merely fastened onto other, newer sports, whether or not such behavior had any use or meaning, and here it continued to flourish as if it had a life of its own.

The accelerating technology that had made war more terrible had also brought new weapons into the sportsman's arsenal: reliable shotguns for fowlers, split-cane rods, waterproof silk lines, and light-eyed hooks for anglers. These advances made bird-shooting and fishing true sports, and even if these gentler activities didn't need rigid rules, the rising middle class that began taking to the fields and streams most certainly did. They were not to be cheated out of the delicious agonies of etiquette simply because the age of elegance had passed. They would do the proper thing at any cost, and archaic posturing made a pursuit just that much more "pukka."

Hardly more than a hundred years ago, these sports — in their modern forms — were still new. It was not long ago, for example, that game birds that had escaped the stoop of the falcon were rather crudely butchered for food after teams of spaniels drove the birds to nets. It was a far cry from the ritual of a modern Scottish grouse shoot. Fishing, too, had long been considered only a pleasant food-gathering activity. The revered Izaak Walton used live baits for all kinds of fishing quite unabashedly, and his *Compleat Angler* is more a picture of pastoral enjoyment than of formal sport.

Young queen Victoria and her friends found diversion in spearing salmon by torchlight on the rivers of her Scottish estates; this now-heinous activity was thought quite proper until the middle of her reign.

Even after the outlawing of salmon-spearing, salmon fisheries escaped the full force of the onrushing "sporting revolution" because salmon rivers were the jealously guarded properties of the nobility. To this day in Europe there is no stigma attached to using spoons, spinners, wobbling plugs, or even minnows, prawns, and worms sewn onto a murderous gaggle of treble hooks when angling for salmon — practices that would get you thrown off any decent trout water on any other continent.

Until Victorian times, a trout fishery was not considered to be of much value. The harvest of trout and other fish by countrymen was tolerated as long as the noble salmon was left alone, just as the gamekeeper might wink at a snared rabbit or two as long as

A century ago, fly-fishing on private Long Island preserves was a social

the hares, gamebirds, and stags were not molested. And yet this lesser fish, the trout, was to become the prime quarry, not only because it was more accessible to the new sportsman but because a trout feeds more on stream-bred insects — and is therefore more catchable on small artificial flies with fine tackle — than any other game fish of decent size.

And this is what modern trout fishing is all about: delicacy, refinement, artistry. Few anglers aspire to catching a blue whale on a power winch. But to take a five-pound trout on an artificial fly less than a quarter-inch long and tied to a leader that will break under a pound of pull — now that's an accomplishment. The

ritual. Elegant clothes were part of the scene.

trout's preference for an insect diet makes this feat a distinct possibility, while a pike, bluefish, or barracuda of similar size wouldn't even notice such a token lure.

Fortunately, the trout's habitat is populated by thousands of species of insects that spend most of their lives in or above or under the water. The mosquito and the mini-vampire black fly of the North Woods are probably the best-known members of this group because they bite innocent non-fishermen. The vast majority of these insects, however, such as the mayflies, caddis flies, and stone flies are fragile, harmless, delicious (to trout), and are recognized only by dedicated flyfishers and entomologists.

These insects spend ninety-nine percent of their lives in underwater forms, hiding under stones and debris, living on algae and other small organisms while breathing through external gills. Once they are fully grown, they swim, crawl, or float to the surface, split their skins, and emerge suddenly and miraculously as glistening, winged insects. In this form they take to the air, breed, lay eggs, and die in a few brief hours or, at most, days. Although the trip to the surface and the float downstream before take-off may require only seconds after a full year of grubbing and growing on the stream-bottom, this is the time when trout feed on them with abandon. When many flies are hatching out at the same time, as is often the case, a passable imitation of these small, delicate insects concocted out of fur and feathers can be very effective indeed.

And this is the ritual of modern fly-fishing. Insects are collected, studied, counterfeited, and presented on ultrarefined tackle. Outwitting the fish with cunningly contrived artificials is more important than the size or the quantity of the catch. Yet the game didn't start this way at all. The use of artificial flies for trout goes back nearly two thousand years, though it is seldom remembered that the original invention was in no way an affectation. The aquatic insects on which trout feed are simply too small and fragile to remain impaled on a hook when they are flung out over a river and so ersatz flies were devised that could take more punishment.

Primitive flies, or those in general use until the miracles of modern metallurgy came to the rescue, had to be fished "wet," or under the surface. When fish were seen snatching adult, winged insects directly off the surface, these primitive artificials may have been dangled or dapped on the water surface below the tip of a long rod, but the fly itself did not, and could not, float.

All this began to change when someone discovered that, by using the stiffest, most waterproof feathers (fighting-cock hackles) and ultralight hooks, flies could exploit the phenomenon of surface tension and float by themselves. The first printed record of this development occurs in 1841, but it wasn't until 1886 when Frederick M. Halford published *Floating Flies and How to Dress Them* that the dry—or floating—fly reached the world at large.

The most significant entomological discovery of the nineteenth century — to proper Victorians, at least — was not the malaria mosquito or the tsetse fly, but the dry fly that was pioneered on the chalkstreams of Hampshire. And its concept, its form, its manner of presentation, its every aspect was infused with the attitudes of the proper English gentleman. Even now there lingers an ultrapurist school of fly-fishing that offers a curious kind of snob-appeal to those who were not to the manor born. The Halfordian dry fly was very much a blue-nosed fly, a change-resistant emblem of what was then a new sporting peerage, a new but congenitally conservative fishing establishment.

Halford was an English gentleman who had fished with the less-remembered men who had pioneered this technique for trout: Henry Sinclair Hall, Dr. Thomas Sanctuary and George Selwyn Marryat. Halford was so taken with the beauty and delicacy of this new sport that he forsook money-grubbing in all its forms at a relatively young age to devote his life to the perfection and promulgation of the dry fly. Though his only original contributions to fly-fishing were several sets of exquisite and increasingly refined dry-fly patterns, his voice was soon considered second only to thunder over Mount Sinai.

As chief spokesman for dry-fly practice and its exclusive use, Halford laid out the rules in no uncertain terms. It was damnably thoughtless, he argued, for a chap to wade down the center of a stream setting up a miniature tidal wave and thrashing the water, left and right, with a team of wet, or sunk, flies and then ripping them back through the current. This time-honored practice might work at times, but it appealed to the noble trout's baser instincts,

A floating mayfly imitation tied with split, quill-section wings in the classic Halford manner. Still a killing fly.

it ruined the next angler's chances by frightening the fish, and it lightly hooked and lost many fish that would soon become so suspicious as to be virtually uncatchable.

The drill every gentleman should follow out of respect for both fish and fellow-fishermen, Halford argued, was the following. The angler should walk slowly along the stream-bank (no wading) until he saw a trout breaking the surface by feeding regularly on mature, winged insects that were floating overhead. A sample of the species of fly being taken should be captured, identified and an exact (as nearly as possible) imitation should be knotted onto the fine, tapered leader.

Now, from a carefully chosen position on the bank (preferably a kneeling one to avoid detection), the angler should cast this counterfeit in an upstream direction so that it will alight delicately a few feet directly up-current of the trout's feeding position. The upstream direction of casting is pivotal, for the fly must now float down-current completely unimpeded by the attached leader and line, just as the natural flies have been doing.

If there are any disruptive, intervening tongues of current between the angler and his fly, a further refinement in technique must be added to ensure a "dead-drift" presentation. The line must, in this event, be made to land in a curve, or in a series of curves, so that the resulting slack must first be straightened out before the pull of the line can exert itself—thus allowing the fly

The more impressionistic fly advocated by the Catskill school of tyers after Gordon. Wings, veiled by hackle, seem to buzz.

time to drift over the trout's nose before it is dragged unnaturally off course. The recipe ends up: Repeat at regular intervals until the fish grows suspicious and stops rising or makes a fatal mistake in judgment due to the flyfisher's (or fly-tyer's) consummate artistry.

To anyone who has ever yanked a hapless sunfish out of a pond on a hunk of worm threaded onto a penny hook, the imperatives of this method make the Ten Commandments seem as permissive as *laissez-faire*. Consider for a moment the "Thou-shalt-nots" this technique imposes.

First, you must *not* pay any mind to trout feeding underwater, but rather locate a fish feeding regularly on surface flies. Second, you must cast only to this fish and *not* prospect in likely places. Third, you must *not* appeal to the fish's carnal instincts by pitching in a succulent worm, minnow, crawfish, or any imitation of these. Fourth, you must *not* merely observe the general type of insect present in the habitat but must ascertain which species of fly and preferably which sex of this species (there are usually slight size and color differences between males and females) the fish is taking. Fifth, you must *not* concoct any impressionistic artificial that could represent a general type, for only an exact replica of this insect of the moment may be knotted onto your leader. Sixth, you must *not* multiply your chances by using two or more flies. Seventh, you must *not* better your casting position or angle of attack by now entering the water. Eighth, you must *not* let the situation dictate your angle of attack—your presentation— for your fly must be cast in an upstream direction. Ninth, it must *not* dip underwater but must be presented "dry," or on the surface only. Tenth, it must *not* be jiggled to attract the trout's attention or manipulated in any way to cater to the trout's killer instinct. Anything but dead drift is bad form and utterly unmannerly.

Can you imagine a longer or more blue-nosed list of blue laws? And would you consider applying them all to the pastoral pastime that Walton called "the blameless sport"? Yet this is precisely what the authorities decreed that trout fishing should be, and they were followed for decades.

Admittedly, this ultrarefined method disturbs the water little and it can, indeed, account for some notable catches on the clear chalkstreams where Halford and his friends cast their flies. But this type of water makes up less than two percent of Britain's total trout fisheries and a far smaller percentage in most other trout-producing countries.

These special streams in southern England (and a very few smaller ones across the Channel in Normandy) are unusual examples of the perfect environment for both trout and dry-fly fishers. All the water entering them is filtered through several hundred feet of pure chalk and then metered out from deep springs with a nearly constant flow and temperature, winter or summer, flood or drought. The advantages of this rare type of river system to both fish and their food are phenomenal.

During its six-month travel through the organic chalk, rain water absorbs rich carbonates and other minerals to the maximum of its carrying capacity. As a result, chalkstream water, gallon for gallon, is twenty times as fertile and productive of trout food as water from the average mountain stream. But that's only the beginning.

Since deep springs discharge water that's nearly the same temperature all year around, it's never too hot or too cold to put off the feeding and digestion of the trout or the rapid growth of their insect food. And, because this flow is nearly always constant in volume as well, there are no destructive floods to hurl fish and food downstream, nor are there punishing droughts to diminish the size or the amenity of their habitat. If trout had ever been granted the divine power to create their own promised land, the weed-paved chalkstreams that slide through the water meadows of Hampshire would have more than filled the bill.

These precious few streams were considered paradise by elegant anglers too. One didn't apply for a rod privilege here any more than one invited oneself to a Duke's party. One waited and hoped to be asked. Fishing rights, whether owned outright or leased by a club, seldom changed hands, and when they did the price was likely to be far higher per yard of bank than on even the choicest salmon rivers to the North.

From this trout-fishing Eden, the high priest, Halford, and his acolytes sent out their pronouncements to Wales, Scotland, Canada, New Zealand, America—to all points of the trout-bearing world. Did it matter that northern tribesmen or Colonials had few water-meadow banks, placid pools, hatching mayflies, or rising trout in their tumbling and unfertile mountain streams? Not a whit. A gentleman fished the dry fly for trout, upstream and drag-free, and that was that.

Fashionable Americans in the Northeast, taking their cue from Britain, as was their custom, quickly embraced the floating fly. Large portions of streams and pond-studded forests were leased or bought up by individuals or groups so they could practice their sport without competition from bait or wet-fly fishers.

In the early years of this movement, before lodges and summer residences had been completed, elite New Yorkers worked out an exclusive system for trout fishing without tears. On Friday nights these gentlemen would dine elegantly at Delmonico's and then head for Grand Central Station where a special Pullman car had been reserved. Here they bedded down, presumably at a reasonable hour, and slept while their hotel on wheels was taxied up to the Catskills or Adirondacks and parked on a siding. This was their clubhouse for the weekend and, on Sunday night, they were towed back to the city in time to appear at their brokerages or businesses at the proper hour on Monday morning. No traffic, no wear-and-tear.

Many of these estates and clubs exist intact to this day. The dry-fly code is still followed on many choice, private sections of New York and Pennsylvania streams where sunk-fly fishing in any form is looked upon as a mucker's or fish-monger's game.

In defense of Halford, it must be noted that he never con-
demned the use of the sunk fly as categorically as his followers did
(at least not in print) and the excesses that ensued may have been
due more to the fanaticism of the disciples than to the preachings

Frederick M. Halford was the supreme authority for three decades.
His pronouncements rivaled those from Mt. Sinai.

Although he went to all the right schools—
and rivers—Skues was pitched out for one
small deviation from Halfordism.

of the master. Whatever its origin, dry-fly exclusivity became an
ethical issue and the wet-fly forces, despite occasional rebuttals
from the North Country and the Colonies, were excoriated in
issue after issue of *The Fishing Gazette* and in the elite Journal of
*The Fly-Fisher's Club* of London. Purists quickly gained the upper
hand, for theirs was obviously a position of superior moral
rectitude.

Then, in 1910, when the Halfordians were at the peak of their
power with no new worlds to conquer, a man in Halford's peer
group and one who also fished the chalkstreams began to rally the
routed wet-fly anglers. In that year, G.E.M. Skues published
*Minor Tactics of the Chalk Stream* pointing out what the trout's
stomach contents had proclaimed for years: Trout take over
ninety percent of their insect food in its underwater, or nymphal,
form and less than ten percent as winged adults off the surface.
Why not, Skues proposed, cast an exact imitation of the various
mayfly nymphs to fish that were seen feeding on the naturals
rising toward the surface to hatch?

Consider, for a moment, the modesty of this proposal. Skues

had no intention of flogging the water indiscriminately, and he agreed to cast only to fish seen feeding actively on insects. He didn't ask license to wade. He promised to present only an exact imitation of the nymph in question—not the old, winged wet fly that was considered a lure or at best a nondescript—and he agreed to fish it drag-free or without any enticing motion. But couldn't he just fish it slightly *below* the surface film where trout took ninety percent of their insect food instead of on top?

He most certainly could not!

The battle raged anew. Sunk-flyfishers came out of hiding to rally around their champion. But the establishment had the last word and it was a crushing one. Poor Skues was forced to resign his rod-privilege on a choice river (for which he had been paying a handsome annual fee) and was exiled to find his fishing wherever he could!

World War I, which was then looming, changed Britain beyond all recognition—at least from a Victorian point of view. And World War II, a cruelly few years later, ushered in an era of even more accelerated change. Today the thrust of English angling innovation and literature has turned toward still-water trout fishing on the many new reservoirs and hydroelectric impoundments. Modern British trout books concentrate on midge pupae, diving beetles, stickleback minnows, and the like—a ragtag assortment of sunk flies that would have shocked even the liberal nymphman, Skues.

The chalkstreams are still there, of course. Their clear, cool, fertile waters continue to flow over beds of curling waterweed, and they are still the choicest, most expensive trout waters in the world. But they no longer dominate trout-fishing thought and theory. Not in Britain nor anywhere else.

Today, Halford's grandson lives in the valley of his ancestor's beloved River Test—the greatest of the chalkstreams. Skues left no descendants. But his spirit would be content in this valley. His appeal for a more sensible fly-fishing policy had already begun to prevail before his death in 1949. His once-radical theory is accepted establishment doctrine now.

You will be told about this if you're ever invited to fish one of the great chalkstreams (though your chances of this are still slim, no matter whom you know). The fishery rules have been changed slightly, yet significantly, since Halford's day to read: "No wading. Dry fly *and nymph* only."

*And nymph?* Yes, British purism is no longer ramrod rigid. It has bent a bit in response to the fishing realities of the present century. And who knows how permissive it may become in another fifty years? Perhaps a new pundit will arise and "discover" what his great grandfather took for granted: that the classic, down-winged sunk fly is actually the best possible imitation of a drowned mayfly or caddis fly. Then, perhaps, the 2,000-year-old wet fly will be considered respectable and will be countenanced on these holy waters, too. And we'll be right back where we started.

# 17

## More Trout Per Mile

Trout fishing that lies within one-day driving distance of our population centers is mostly bad and, let's face it, getting worse. Unfortunately, the situation is much like the weather in Mark Twain's day: Everybody talks about it, but nobody does anything about it.

Admittedly, sportsmen's groups, state governments, and private owners pour a lot of hatchery trout into our Eastern streams. But most of these innocents find few places to hide and have little chance for long-term survival. For example, a lady of my acquaintance who owns a stretch of small stream lost all her spring stocking, a few years ago, due to a late-May flood. Undaunted, she ordered another batch for the end of June. By this time, the water was catastrophically low and, when the fish were dumped in, she and the hatchery man watched in horror as $500 worth of trout stampeded downstream like a school of bonefish, never to be seen again.

Stocked fish may not always be such a sudden and total loss, but it's a dubious policy to try to stockpile trout where they don't want to live. Hatchery fish are expensive, too. Perhaps trout fanciers should take a tip from suburban birdwatchers. When the binocular boys want to attract and hold song birds, they plant protective shrubs or bushes and set out bird houses. Why shouldn't trouters build trout houses on their favorite streams?

What our run-down running waters really need is not more trout but more trout-holding places. Much has been learned and written about improving the richer, more stately flowing streams of the upper Midwest. Yet the problems of the acid, rocky spate rivers of the East have been largely neglected — despite the fact that these are the very waters that support the most fishermen and the fewest trout per mile.

Our larger streams — those that are eighty feet or more wide — are able to sustain fair fishing through sheer volume of water and depth, even when they are severely damaged. Smaller streams and brooks, however, show the effects of erosion more dramatically. And these cooler waters, which start nearer the springs and flow at higher altitudes, are the mainstays of both our summer fishing and our resident watershed trout populations. They, in particular, need all the help they can get. The question is, what sort of help?

The solution lies first in finding out what fish-producing characteristics these waters used to have before they were trampled by civilization, and then restoring them. When old-timers tell you about all the big fish they used to catch from your favorite stream, they're not necessarily lying.

A picture pool with rock-cliff sides and boulder-strewn bottom. No need to try to improve on nature here.

Timbering and farming started our streams on their downward path. Thinning, even stripping, our watersheds of trees has caused not only pronounced summer droughts, but destructive floods as well. Perhaps stream-beds could have handled this challenge if they had been left intact. But the banks came tumbling down when farmers tried to stretch their acres by removing trees right down to the edge of the stream.

Once the climax trees, with their massive root structures, were removed, floods began to tear out the margins. If you've ever watched a large tree, with its twelve-foot-diameter root structure, plow its way down a swollen stream-bed you'll understand why so many river banks are now composed of shallow, treeless gravel. After years of this chain-reaction bulldozing and uprooting, most of our running waters are two streams wide and half a stream deep.

When you examine the resulting shallow, unproductive flats (no longer pools) and riffles (no longer runs), the remedy may seem deceptively simple. You'll probably suggest that a dam, raising the water level two or three feet, could make the whole stretch into a promised land.

But you'd be wrong on four counts. First, effective dams are damnably expensive. In many areas, a Hewitt ramp-dam sixty to eighty feet wide may cost several thousand dollars. Second, dams tend to heat up water, making it intolerable to trout. Third, there's now so much unstable sand and gravel in most streams that it will soon fill in your dream pool above the dam, leaving only the limited plunge-pool below for fish-holding. And fourth, damming creates slow water which produces only one-tenth as much food per square foot of bottom as running water does. Eastern spate streams, by their character and chemistry, are food-short to begin with, and we shouldn't reduce their larders even further.

The answer lies, not in direct confrontation with the current, but in using its sudden, destructive power to heal the stream. As a *jujitsu* expert converts his opponent's strength to his own advantage, you can make a river's floods serve your purpose. You can, that is, if you use the proper techniques.

During the past thirteen summers I have spent at least as much time tinkering with running water as I've spent fishing it and over

Flat, shallow water has been speeded up by cribbing (right) which is soon deeply undercut and will hold large trout.

that period I've made all the obvious mistakes. On the other hand, I have had a few heartening successes, and if you think catching a fish on a fly you tied yourself is a thrill, just wait till you take a good trout from a productive spot you've created out of waste water with your own two hands.

I'll discuss several other improvement schemes later on, but first I'd like to describe the most versatile and durable stream-improvement device I've ever seen: the log cribbing. Essentially, this is a low-lying structure of horizontally placed logs anchored securely into the bank on the upstream end, jutting out into the current below, and ballasted with large rocks for flood insurance. Although the cribbing is far from new and I certainly didn't invent it, I may have improved it some.

Careful planning and foresight must go into the positioning of these structures. They should be built only on the strong side of

Lower logs and screening in place for simple cribbing. Be sure to place the biggest rocks nearest the logs.

Same cribbing completed, two logs high and ballasted against flood-waters. Willow roots soon make it a permanent peninsula.

the current or at least where they will be nearest to the dominant feed-lane. Don't place them over ledge-rock — no matter how permanent such a location may appear to be. A cribbing can't possibly scour fish-holding undercuts there, and trout don't like to lie over uninterrupted sheet-rock, anyway. Choose a place with a gravel or rubble bottom in a shallow riffle or unproductive flat.

Pivotal to your future success is the embedding of the first log — the bottom one on the upstream end. It must be dug into the bank or neighboring gravel deeply enough — two or three feet on tight, tree-lined banks, but up to six or eight feet on unstable, shelving shores — so that high waters can't work in behind it and scour it out. At this stage, a little extra digging is money in the bank; and it will help you sleep better during those nights later on when the river is in flood.

Logs should be of hemlock, larch, or cedar — woods that can withstand alternate wetting and drying without rotting. Pine is virtually useless, and even the choicest hardwoods will disintegrate in a few seasons if they're not totally submerged all the time. Hemlock is usually easy to get in most parts of the Northeast, and it's light enough to handle. Twenty-foot logs measuring a foot across the butt can be moved short distances by one man with a crowbar or cant hook and are the best all-round size. Try to select smooth-trunked and knot-free logs so that debris won't find a place to hang up. Finally, before you lower the first one into its resting-place, slice the downstream end in half and remove the top section for twelve to eighteen inches much as you would in building a log cabin. This will allow the next log, if a bottom section is removed, to fit in like one continuous log.

Before filling in the trench you have imbedded the end of this log in, cut some willow switches slightly longer than the final depth of burial and poke their butts in as far as possible along both sides of the log. Willows planted in saturated sand or gravel are almost sure to take and, once established, are great insurance against the loss of this key log.

The face of the cribbing formed by this log should be slanted out into the current at an angle of no more than forty-five degrees and in some cases as little as thirty degrees, depending on the location. Large cakes of ice or whole trees tend to hang up on structures that confront the flood waters too directly, while more gradual inclines will shrug off menacing objects, deflecting them harmlessly down-current.

Whether you build a simple or complex cribbing will depend on the location you have chosen. A complex cribbing is merely one that is continued down-current with a second section jutting out into the current at a sharper angle. Construction principles are essentially the same, but a simple one is sooner completed and may make a better choice for your first efforts. The complex one may hold twice as many trout, but only in special situations—either at a bend in the river or below a diagonal riffle where the current angles sharply towards one bank. (On a straight stretch, this longer structure would have to jut out perilously far into the river and the angle of the second log, to continue the current deflection, would have to be placed at nearly ninety degrees to the flow.)

The second log, which forms the lower arm of a simple cribbing (which is just a widened A-frame skeleton) should be equally well trenched and anchored into the bank, then mortised and spiked into the first one. To be sure you won't lose your future rock ballast when the cribbing has been deeply undercut by high water, attach heavy-gauge, wide-mesh (eight-inch or more) wire fencing of four-foot or more width to the inside of these logs before you start to pile on the rocks. Fasten at six-inch intervals with either the largest-size staples or three-inch nails. If you use nails, bend the top inch down over the wire.

Next, place the heaviest rocks available on the part of the fencing that's nearest the logs, laying two rows horizontally. Be sure they're too large to fall through the wire mesh, and the bigger the better. Pull these rocks out of the nearby water, never from the bank which needs all the protection it can get. Removing them from within a few feet of the face of the cribbing helps in another way, too. It reduces the stability of that portion of the stream-bottom, helping the current to scour deeper and to produce a more pronounced cut for fish-holding.

The upper layer of logs should be placed exactly on top of the first and fastened in the same manner—except that a second layer of wire is seldom necessary. Top logs should barely break the surface even at low water so that most flood-borne objects will

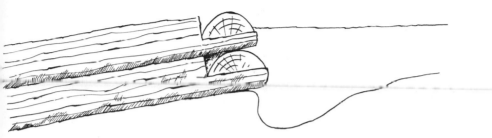

Side view from water level of newly finished cribbing.

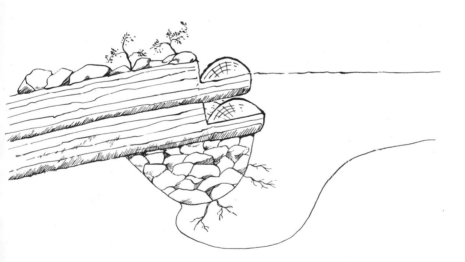

Same cribbing after high water has created deep undercut.

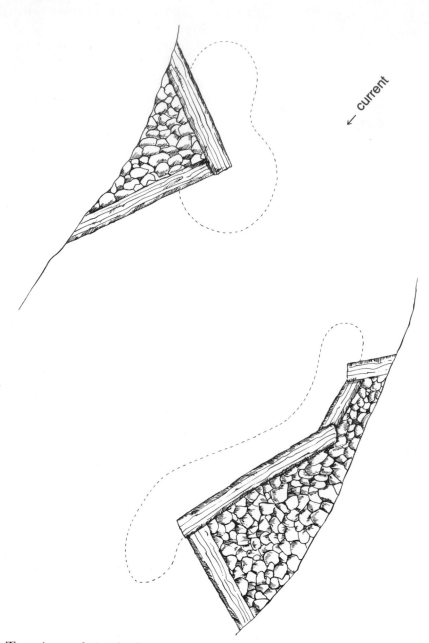

Top views of simple (left) and complex cribbings. Areas inside dotted lines will soon be scoured deep by floods.

pass over them. This final position has to be precalculated when digging the trenches for the lower logs.

Once again, place the largest rocks you can handle adjacent to the logs, then slant the rock-fill back so it is higher near the bank. It will pay you to fit the big, marginal rocks as carefully as you would a dry wall, for they, too, will have to shed high-water flotsam. Finally, plant willow shoots in the rock interstices all over the cribbing and repeat this every spring until you have a dense stand established. In two or three years, these fast-growing plants will catch debris with their trunks and branches and actually increase current deflection in high water. This not only adds to the scouring action, but also helps force destructive objects to swerve away from your cribbing.

Properly positioned, constructed, and planted, a cribbing should last for many years with only minor maintenance or repairs. Several that I have built on a good-sized river in New York's Catskills came through the Act-of-God flood of the summer of '69 with flying colors. However, less well-conceived and built structures from earlier experiments were lost, and this experience has given me some insight into which improvement schemes will—and which will not—stand up.

Gabions (fine-mesh wire cages filled with rocks) have very little value as improvers of flood-prone streams. When they deflect enough water to scour a good trench, they tumble into their own handiwork and disappear. They just aren't rigid enough to withstand much undercutting.

Simple deflector and current-directing logs that have proved themselves on more stable waters won't work here, either. They may produce the desired effect at low or medium flow, but under full flood conditions the water roars over them and attacks the bank behind them, increasing the destruction. The inflexible law that water will run off at a precise right angle to any surface it flows over is the very reason why down-current ends of all cribbings must be finished off at an obtuse — never an acute — angle to the bank.

There are, however, some less Herculean labors you can perform for a stream that will help it little by little. Willow-planting along banks is always good practice since these small trees are water-loving and strong-rooted. Riprapping the sand banks

Driving in a spike for willow-planting on an eroded shore. Nature may heal herself, but you can hurry the process.

with large, flat slabs can halt further erosion and siltation downstream.

Large rocks and boulders are always a welcome addition to a stream-bed, but the biggest you can roll are barely big enough. By all means don't steal them from the nearby banks. Large boulders usually produce short, deep scours on their down-current side while insect-food debris—dead leaves and twigs—will tend to catch under their front edges.

If you and your friends or your club decide to try to help your favorite streams, there are certain procedures you should follow. Ask permission from your state fish and game commission before you start. Many require permits to tamper with flowing water — even if you're the riparian owner. However, if your plans are sound, they'll usually give you their blessing and often some helpful advice.

If you lease the water or merely have permission to fish it, by all means get the owner's approval as well. Again, if your projects offer real improvement, he can hardly object.

When you've been given the go-ahead, resist the temptation to rush into construction. First, draw up a master plan for the area you're going to improve. Observe and take notes on this water at least once when it is in flood or running extremely high. This will not only impress you with the forces your future structures will have to contend with, but it may also give you a whole new understanding of which direction the river tends to cut when it's actually working. And there's much to be learned from studying productive pools and runs, even in low water, analyzing the high-water forces that dug them and keep them scoured clean.

Finally, start your first project at a tight-banked, relatively stable location. It's heartbreaking to slave over a cribbing only to discover, the following season, that the river has cut itself a new channel, leaving your good works high and dry on the gravel. For the same reason, work in a progressive downstream direction. Your first cribbing may deflect the current to the opposite bank and it's vital to know this before starting your next structure.

I have built several cribbings singlehandedly (despite what my children and weekend guests may tell you), but extra hands make the work quicker and pleasanter. Machinery can do wonders if

Rock-ballasting by the highway department on the far shore holds riverbank and trout. Rocks must be five-hundred pounds or more.

you're willing to pay the price. A back-hoe can dig deep trenches in a short time and a payloader can pile on all the ballast you'll need (*after* you've hand-fitted the big, outside rocks) in a few hours. With this sort of help — and expense — it's possible to complete an entire cribbing in a single day if you have pre-arranged all the materials and planned the construction sequence properly.

What sort of return, in terms of actual fish, can you expect from the finished product? It all depends on the stream you're working with and on the existing head of fish in the river available for attraction. Even a simple cribbing can hold several good (over 12-inch) fish despite the territorial aggressiveness of trout. On a rare, perfect evening, I have caught five in a row without moving my feet from one such structure, and I'm not sure there weren't even more that were put down before I could cover them. A compound cribbing, as I've said, may hold twice as many.

My all-time favorite fishing place was created by this latter type of structure. Facing upstream from where I like to stand, the water breaks over a diagonal riffle which bunches the thread of the current sharply toward the bank to my right. While the water is still dancing and deepening, it meets the first log which angles out slightly from the bank. The flow hugs this log for twenty feet or more, slowing down into a smooth glide, then hits the second log which juts out more sharply. The current gradually quickens again until it boils out past the end of this last log and shallows out into another riffle. For nearly fifty feet, the water near the logs is three to three and a half feet deep and it fishes like a short pool in low water, like a deep run when the river's up.

This place has everything a trout could ask for. There's a food-producing riffle directly above, a concentrated feed lane of drift food, and cover enough under the logs and between the rocks to hide even some full-grown salmon. It's ideal for the fisherman, too. Your presentations here are almost drag-free, for the current moves past you like a turning wheel—slowest at the hub where you stand and fastest out on the rim where your fly is cast.

Cribbings have one other big advantage: They can stretch the length of your good-fishing season. Brown trout have two main migration periods. They move upstream for cooler water and safer depths during the first hint of drought in early summer. A good undercut can hold some of these fish all summer, keeping them from pushing on through to spring-holes and feeder creeks. And in the fall, during September and October, all the mature fish in the stream seem to play musical chairs. Your fishing season may now be over, but cribbings provide ideal wintering spots and will hold large fish upriver for your early-spring fishing. These big trout might otherwise head down to the big water after spawning.

Is this sort of work worth all the backaches and blisters? It all depends on your available time, temperament, and long-range commitment to trout fishing. The number of fishermen is increasing every year by leaps and bounds while the amount of available trout water is probably shrinking. Don't let the antipollution bills —good as they are—mislead you. Even if they're carried out to the letter, they will do far more to reclaim larger rivers for warm-water species than they will to expand upland trout waters. In the meantime, we'll probably keep losing water to the dammers and developers.

Probably every generation has complained about the fishing, wishing for the good old days. An Elizabethan poet 375 years ago wrote:

> Fishing, if I, a fisher, may protest
> Of pleasures is the sweetest, of sports the best, . . .
> But now the sport is marde, and wott ye why?
> Fishes decrease, and fishers multiply.

He had no idea how good he had it! But lamenting and viewing-with-alarm are no answer. Obviously, as a trout fisherman, you should support all good conservation measures and ecology-minded candidates. Certainly you should join Trout Unlimited, the Federation of Fly Fishermen, and any organization dedicated to the future of your sport.

But perhaps you should get even more deeply involved with some local grass-roots — or rather, willow-roots — work on your favorite stream. This is the only way to produce more trout per existing mile of stream. And, if you shuttle the current back and forth from bank to bank artfully enough, you just might create a few more miles of trout fishing, too.

# A Dry-Fly Philosophy

Socrates gave his wife all the credit for his success as a philosopher, but not in the usual I-owe-it-all-to-the-little-lady sense. He claimed Xanthippe was such a shrew and all-around five-letter girl that she had driven him into the arms of abstract thought.

I think Socrates was putting us on, though. If his theory held water, sheer frustration would also drive dry-fly fishermen to embrace pure logic and, as a result, they would surely quit fishing. Instead, they head for the stream at every opportunity armed with new flies, new theories, and new hopes even though sad experience has proved that for every small sip of success there are many cupfuls of hemlock to be choked down. I always get depressed by the top-heavy failure/success ratio when I reread my own fishing diary, and the disastrous day of July 5, 1964, is a typical example.

The previous evening had set me up for the coming defeat. In the hour before pitch darkness I had raised, pricked, or caught every rising fish I had cast to with a new imitation of a pale-yellowish dun that had long been one of the most baffling hatches on my river. I was especially pleased with this performance because the sudden-death imitation had been created in the classic manner — duplicated from live, captured specimens. I won't go into the whole dressing, for reasons that will soon become obvious, but the major change I had made from previous recipes was in the body, where I had substituted porcupine hair dyed the color of creamery butter for the usual, much duller fox-belly fur. With this inspired concoction I had given a dozen and a half trout a good toothache before darkness and a sudden downpour had driven me from the river.

By the next day, the infamous 5th of July, the river had risen six inches and, since it was still drizzling, I spent most of the morning tying up a boxful of my new "Yellow Perils." The sun came out at two o'clock and by four I was on the river—playing a hunch that cooling rainwater might start the flies hatching several hours early.

Again, my touch was pure magic. At four-thirty the same pale-yellow duns started pouring down my favorite flat and despite the bright sunlight the trout came strongly on the feed. This was going to be ridiculously easy. Higher, faster water would make the fish far less shy and I had a whole boxful of my new secret weapons. I fully expected to walk away within an hour, fed up with fishing that was too murderous to be fun.

As it turned out, it was more than three hours later when I finally left the river and my hands hardly smelled fishy. I had caught only two six-inchers and had been totally ignored by all the fish old enough to spawn. What had gone wrong? How could trout have savaged an imitation one evening then acted like militant consumerists when presented with the identical fly the very next day? The higher water, which had actually relieved near-drought conditions, should have been strongly in my favor. The critical difference appeared to be available light — heavily clouded skies at dusk versus bright afternoon sun.

Up to that point, I had thought of light as a basic commodity that could be measured on a simple scale of more or less. After all, an artificial fly in the hand looks much the same to us at dusk as it does in sunlight except for the brightness of the colors. This is true, however, only because we tend to view it in terms of the light it reflects back to our eyes.

Unfortunately, the trout's world and his modes of perception are quite different and far more complicated. He sees a mayfly floating overhead in at least three distinct ways and in many combinations of the three. In extremely poor light the fly probably blocks out all the rays reaching the trout's eyes and appears as a colorless silhouette. In bright sunlight the same insect seems mainly translucent, the light passing through the body, wings, and legs with only slight refraction, and the color of its internal organs may be even more distinctive than the color of its skin. Then, of course, when perceived by reflected light, the fly may look to the trout much as it does to us, but I believe this is only for relatively short periods of time between the translucent and opaque light conditions.

I think this explains my ups and downs on the July 4th and 5th I mentioned earlier. The imitation fooled the fish at dusk because it was being seen by reflected light at first, perhaps, and then as a pure silhouette. However, this same artificial had none of the translucence of the natural when viewed against the bright sky the following day and may well have been passed up as an inedible hemlock needle.

If you hold a live mayfly between your eye and a bright light, then at a right angle to the light and finally against a very dim light, your eye may well convince you that you have been looking at three separate insects, and if you move the fly slowly through all three stages you may see an almost infinite number of gradations in the appearance of that same fly. This nearly duplicates what a trout probably sees during the various hours of a single day and when you consider this enormous variety of perceptions, you may easily, and rightly, despair of ever creating, or finding, the perfect artificial of any insect.

What we often tend to forget is that all dry flies are a compromise between the true appearance of a natural insect and what we can manage to spin on a relatively heavy hook and then float over a fish. Each type, or even tying, of an artificial is based on the premise that some of the things a trout perceives are more important than others in convincing him that this is lean red meat and not just a bundle of fluff. These aspects are emphasized while others, deemed less important, are necessarily sacrificed. With this in mind, let's look at some of the most popular schools of dry-fly tying, restricting our scrutiny to mayfly artificials since, for some inscrutable reason, ninety-nine percent of all floaters sold imitate this form of aquatic insect.

To make things simpler, let's break flies down into their four basic parts: tail, body, hackle, and wing. I'm sure trout don't do this, but fly-tyers do and this piece-by-piece approach helps put some order into centuries of fly-tying chaos.

Tails are the least controversial and worried-over part of the classic dry fly. Many of the most effective wet flies omit them altogether so it's easy to conclude that these hairlike and un-nourishing appendages aren't the focal point of the trout's attention. The earliest dry flies on record sported only two or three whisks — exactly the number of tails (or *setae*) the naturals themselves possess. However, this number was soon increased for practical reasons and, since trout apparently can't count, the more fully fibered tails are the norm today.

Don't let this mislead you into thinking that tails are just so much excess baggage, though. These few fibers are called upon to support and float nearly two-thirds of the total hook-weight — the heaviest portion over the bend and barb — and a short, sparse tail can condemn the rear end of a floater to sink below the surface film and leave your imitation pitched at an improbable angle. To prevent this, I tie my flies with the tail fibers splayed out in a horizontal fan, spreading thirty to forty degrees, the way most naturals flair their tails. I have no great faith that trout appreciate this small gesture towards realism, but this does help prevent tail-sinking and it has other advantages, too. This fanned-out position offers much more air resistance and helps the imitation flutter down to the surface in the horizontal plane we hope for. And, since the fibers are spread out perpendicular to the hook-bend, it helps to cock the fly in a bolt-upright position once it hits the water.

Many years ago I showed one of our most famous fly-tyers a series I had tied up in this manner, asking his professional appraisal. "Sure it floats a fly better, and presents it better, too. We've known that for years," he added, dashing my hopes for immortality as the Thomas Edison of fly-tying. "But they'd never sell. People expect flies to have a straight, bunched tail and that's what they get." He was right, of course. I have since seen fan-tailed flies illustrated in books and articles, but I have never seen them offered in tackle shops. However, I think it will pay you to tie up some flies like this or to get a friend to create some for you. They're that much better.

When we come to fly bodies we enter the eye of a storm that has been raging for centuries. The first dry flies had spun-fur bodies as did the ancient wet patterns described by Charles Cotton in *The Compleat Angler*. Nearly ninety years ago, Frederick M. Halford, the English genius who launched and popularized the dry fly, decided that these fuzzy-bodied imitations weren't realistic enough—at least not from a photographic point of view. In line with his doctrine of "exact imitation" he redesigned these flies with glistening, segmented bodies of horsehair dyed to a precise color. Although these same patterns are sold and used on Britain's chalkstreams to this day, the pendulum has swung back toward the older style in recent years and you now have a wide choice of body-types in even shop-tied flies.

One of the more interesting rebuttals to Halford's hard-nosed theory was launched by an English mathematician in 1924. J. W. Dunne, along with many fellow dry-fly fishers, had long felt that Halford's patterns, though ultrarealistic when viewed under side-lighted conditions, were opaque and lifeless when seen against a strong light. Dunne's "Sunshine" flies were designed with bodies made of a special synthetic fiber wound over a white-painted hook-shank. When these flies were dipped into a flask of special "Sunshine" oil, they suddenly took on both the color and transparency of the naturals.

"Sunshine" flies have not been on the market since World War II, as far as I can tell, but they may have been a giant step in the right direction. Their disappearance from the catalogs was not due to their lack of killing properties, though. Like so many other demonstrably better flies both before and since, they were just too difficult and time-consuming to tie. And the synthetic body-material was extremely fragile. One sharp trout-tooth could unravel and ruin the laborously created body.

Hard bodies of quill, stiff hair, and other opaque materials are still popular. But many tyers have taken the cue from Dunne and developed translucent bodies of simpler, tougher materials. The old fur-dubbings, particularly those spun from the underfur of aquatic mammals, are reasonably water-repellant, show a lifelike sparkle, and allow enough light to refract through their fuzzy margins to give some hint of transparency. Seal's fur is probably the best of all since it has the most lustre and changes color least when wet. This type of body has gained popularity in recent years and so have those made of fine herls, which also give a translucent appearance.

In selecting bodies of this sort it is best to hold them up to the light (preferably when wet) to choose the shade you hope the fish will see. Over three hundred years ago, Charles Cotton pointed out that the only way to tell a fur dubbing's true color was to hold it up to a strong light. It seems to take a discouragingly long time to rediscover what was common knowledge years ago.

There is one situation in which hard, slim quill bodies may be a better choice, though, and that's when imitating the mayfly spinners that fall spent on the surface at dusk. This second, and less important, stage of the mayfly's flying life has a characteristically thinner body than the earlier dun stage and since it is usually viewed against the fading light of late evening, a slim body of durable quill or hair may present a more realistic silhouette. You can usually discount the factor of translucence under such light conditions. Remember Gilbert and Sullivan's description of the rich attorney's elderly ugly daughter? "She'd well pass for forty-three in the dusk with the light behind her." You, too, can probably fool a poor fish under these flattering conditions, but I doubt that you'd want to be wed to that style of tying for the harsh, unforgiving light of midday.

Hackle is the most important part of any dry fly as far as keeping it afloat is concerned. In classic theory, it is supposed to represent the legs of the insect, but that isn't necessarily the case in modern practice. Spiders, variants, bivisibles, and conventional wingless patterns use hackle to represent both legs and wings and so, in part, do some of the most famous Catskill patterns like the Quill Gordon and the Hendrickson. The wings of bunched wood-duck fibers in these popular patterns are not at all the color of the mayflies' wings they are supposed to imitate. These barred yellow feathers are used to represent the venation of the wings, and their true gray color is recreated only when they are viewed through many turns of dun hackle.

All-hackle flies are popular because they are tough and are high floaters. This latter quality makes them ideal for prospecting in fast runs or in swirling pockets, but I find they're only so-so on the glassy surfaces of pools or flats. Here trout often drift back

The Quill Gordon (Epeorus pleuralis) with impressionistic wings and hackle as tied by the Catskill school . . .

. . . with quill-section wings in the Halford manner . . .

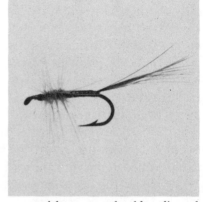

. . . with Baigent's long, watery outer-hackle . . .

. . . with sparse hackle clipped for a spent fly. . .

. . . with Marinaro's splayed hackle and formed wings . . .

. . . as a long-hackled, Catskill-style variant . . .

... as a no-hackle tie with buoyant body-dubbing . . .

. . . and as a parachute fly with horizontally-wound hackle.

under a fly for quite a ways before taking it, and these more stylized patterns are often rejected when studied by good-sized, heavily fished trout.

An interesting attempt at creating a high-floating yet realistic imitation was launched by an Englishman, Dr. Baigent, in the early part of this century. The good doctor must have had a bit of the advertising man in him since he named them "Refractra" flies. They looked much like the standard British dressings of his day with this difference: One short hackle only was used to represent the legs while a second hackle, two or three times as long in the fiber and of a neutral shade, was wound over this, giving a high-floating fly without the usual appearance of too much bulk.

According to Baigent, they had another great advantage. The long, nearly invisible over-hackle produced dimples in the surface-tension over a wider area, creating extra distortion and refraction so that even the most sophisticated trout couldn't get a sharp look at the fly.

The concept of these flies, like Dunne's "Sunshine" theory, is excellent, and the only reason I can imagine for their disappearance from our inventories is the scarcity of the good-quality, pale-dun hackle needed to create the desired illusion. "Refractra" flies have all the good floating qualities of our standard variants and are far more killing on smooth, slow water. I can only hope that with our accelerated interest in new theories and new patterns that someone will "discover" them again very soon.

Believers in all-hackle flies are convinced that no artificial can fool a trout when it can be seen clearly and that it is mainly the sparkles and dimples set up in the surface tension by the hackle points, creating much the same patterns made by an insect's legs, that deceive the fish. There's considerable evidence to support this premise. Until an artificial enters a trout's relatively small window or direct, above-surface vision, these twinkles in the mirror-like water surface give the fish his only advance warning of approaching food. This stimulus seems sufficient in fast or turbulent water where trout are forced into making a hair-trigger decision but, in my experience, it leaves something to be desired when the water is slow and slick.

Vincent Marinaro, of Pennsylvania's limestone country, has come up with an ingenious compromise: a type of fly that should produce a more realistic light pattern outside the trout's window yet one that also deceives when viewed directly by the trout. He accomplishes this by splaying the hackle toward the head and tail of the fly when winding it on. This gives the fly two other advantages: more area of surface tension for the hackle to work on and a more accurate representation of the natural fly's spraddled legs.

I don't know why this style of hackling hasn't caught on. Is it because it looks untidy? After all, one of the hallmarks of a well-tied conventional fly is the close, even turn of hackle at the head, and from this criterion Marinaro's tie looks like a botched job. Whether or not this type of hackling offends your esthetic sensibilities, I can assure you that the result is extremely killing— especially in sizes #16 and smaller.

Parachute flies, those with their hackle wound in a horizontal rather than vertical plane, have been on and off the market for over forty years. They, too, spread their hackle over a larger part of the surface the way a mayfly splays its legs. However, they have one distinct drawback. With the hackle wound above the body, as is customary, the body is presented below the surface film which is uncharacteristic of mayflies. It seems a case of win one, lose one, here.

Flies without any hackle at all have reappeared after a number of years and they certainly deserve a long, hard look. One of the most popular and effective British flies of all time, the Gold-ribbed Hare's Ear, has always been tied in this manner, relying on a few picked-out guard hairs for flotation. This fly is still considered the best dry imitation of the Medium Olive Dun—one of the most important spring flies on England's legendary chalkstreams.

No-hackle flies are unquestionably accurate and deadly imitations under the conditions they were designed for. On English chalkstreams, where this tie originated, most naturals are quite small, averaging to sizes #16 and #18, and artificials of this size are quite easy to float with a minimal grip on surface tension. The water is glassy smooth, here, and few presentations are made since only rising fish are cast to. Unfortunately, we have very few rivers in this country with similar conditions and opportunities. Where these do exist, no-hackle flies are superb. However, on our usual, more turbulent waters where steady casting and prospecting for unseen fish is standard practice, these flies won't float long enough or high enough to be practical.

Imitations of spinners, or spent mayflies, are a different matter, of course. These are traditionally fished to rising trout at dusk on glassy water, and we want them to float flush in the surface film. The best of these imitations have always been tied without conventional hackle. The easiest and most effective tie, I've found, is made by winding on one hackle, then clipping off all the top and bottom fibers, but you can produce this same, spent-wing effect in many other ways.

Some sort of wing is usually preferred by anglers who concentrate on slow, clear waters and these upright "sails" of the mayfly dun can be represented in three basic ways. The classic method is with matching slips of primary feathers. A more impressionistic style is created by using split bunches of plumage as many Catskill flies do or by tying in stiff fibers of hair as in the popular Wulff flies. A relatively new school advocates wings formed of whole hackle feathers clipped to a precise mayfly-wing shape.

Using winged flies for slow-water conditions is sound practice. The top of the wing is the first part of a mayfly that a trout can see directly as it starts to enter his window of direct vision. In slow water this preview of the approaching fly may well be the stimulus that starts a fish gliding up to the surface.

Slips of primary quill, from dark to palest dun, will duplicate the wing-color of most flies you'll encounter. On small flies—size #16 and under—these wings are extremely realistic and they are highly visible to both the trout and the angler. This latter advantage is not to be taken lightly when you're trying to keep track of a #18 fly forty or more feet distant on the surface. Many anglers complain that these quill wings are too fragile and that they break up after a fish or two, but if they have been tied on properly (which, admittedly, is not always the case) the parted fibers can usually be zipped back into a solid wing in seconds.

Medium-sized flies (#16s, #14s, and #12s) are logical candidates for clipped-hackle wings. In sizes smaller than these such wings probably represent a lot of hard work that will be appreciated only by the angler. In fact, these wings are so time-consuming to prepare in all sizes that few professional tyers can afford to offer them. On the positive side, they are realistically translucent, tough and, in larger sizes, they are less likely than quill slips to wind up your tippet while casting.

Flies larger than size #12 are probably best tied with bunched-fiber or hair wings. These are less lifelike, of course, but they are also less rigid. Even clipped-hackle wings over a certain size tend to hum and whirr during high-velocity casting, and they may then wind up your tippet like the rubber band in a model airplane. The largest mayflies—the Green Drake, the March Brown and others —are the hardest naturals to imitate successfully, and I feel that winging realistically is only a small part of the problem. Trout act as if they see larger objects in a different manner than they see smaller ones. Their eyes seem able to pick big flies to pieces, and even the most realistic imitations of the larger naturals are taken with regularity only in fast water or when trout are on a feeding spree.

This phenomenon is hard to explain, but is attested to by the century-long struggle of Britain's most gifted theorists and fly-tyers to come up with an effective imitation of their large Green Drake, usually referred to as *The* Mayfly. There are hundreds of different dressings on the market and yet none of them is considered a reliable killer. In my experience, we have the same problem with our largest insects. This difficulty in deceiving trout with larger floating patterns is so pronounced that I doubt that dry-fly fishing would be at all popular if the average aquatic insect were size #8 or #10 instead of size #14 or #16.

When these giants of the insect world are being taken regularly in slow water (where, unfortunately, most of them hatch out) I usually abandon my faith in the sleight of hand of fly-tying. I then put on a higher-floating, but less realistic, variant of similar size and color and give it a slight twitch in an across or upstream direction just before it passes over the rising fish. Easy does it here: just a wiggle. This mini-motion, I've found, is often more effective in convincing the trout that your artificial is a living insect than the most inspired fly-tying efforts.

Many years ago, when I first started tying flies, I dreamed I might someday invent a pattern that no trout could resist. A little experience put an end to that fantasy, but soon another one popped up in its place. Why couldn't I design a floating imitation of, say, the March Brown dun that no fish feeding on the naturals would ever refuse?

My fly box bears witness that I have now given up even this more modest ambition. These days I tie up several imitations of the more common mayflies I expect to see during the daylight hours on the waters I fish. To stay with the March Brown, for example, I now carry some long-hackled variant imitations for fast water or to twitch slightly on flat water when all else fails. I have some standard Art Flick imitations with yellowish-cream bodies that work well most of the time. But some days, when the overhead light is especially bright, I do far better with this same dressing tied with a body of rusty-orange seal's fur that suggests the gut color of the natural instead of its yellow skin color. And yet, even with this battery, I sometimes do so poorly during a good March Brown hatch that I'm convinced I'm still missing a trick—or several.

One reason for this is that light conditions vary widely and constantly. Then, too, entomologists tell us that the aquatic insects themselves change color gradually and continually after they've hatched out. And mayflies of the very same species differ considerably in color — and in size — from one river to another even though they may be hatching out in the same ecological region. The more I learn about insects, flies, and fly-tying, the more certain I become that the one perfect imitation can never exist.

All this conspires to make fly-tying an absorbing occupation of trial and error punctuated by occasional, temporary successes. Many flies, especially those that hatch out during the bright hours of the day, seem to call for several distinct patterns. Larger specimens continue to defy predictable results with any or all imitations. And so far we've only looked into the problems of duplicating adult mayflies. Floating caddis flies, stone flies, midges, and terrestrials have their own sets of problems. And then there's another universe of nymphs, wet-flies, streamers, bucktails, and the other subsurface imitations to look into.

Obviously, trout aren't as gullible as people. You can't fool all of the fish some of the time or even some of the fish all of the time. If you can manage to fool some of the fish some of the time you'll probably be accused of being an expert. Decades of trial and error have forced me to accept this philosophy. It may have helped me *understand* dry-fly problems, but it hasn't helped me *solve* too many of them.

However, from all reports, philosophy didn't help Socrates solve his problems, either. To begin with, he was extremely ugly. After he married, his wife tried to make his life a hell on earth. And when the citizens of Athens told him to drop dead, they meant it literally. Things might have been worse, though. Think of the added grief he'd have gone through if he'd been addicted to dry-fly fishing.

# The Perfect Fish

Although I had been a compulsive fisherman ever since I could walk, I never saw a specimen of "the perfect fish" until I had reached the advanced age of five and a half, going on six. I can still remember that moment. I was standing on a dusty dirt road, peering into a trickle—certainly not a brook—that dribbled out of a culvert, when I noticed a slight movement in the pan-sized pool below.

There couldn't be a fish in *there*, I thought. Fish, in those days, were sudden shadows that disappeared in front of me as I waded through the shallows of seashores and lakes. Then a creature slowly assembled itself in front of my eyes. First, white-tipped pink fins fanning the yellow sand—probably the motion that had caught my eye in the first place. Then, below, a cigar-shaped shadow and above this a dark-green body laced with paler markings. If I close my eyes today I can still see it in glorious full color, hovering there under the midday sun.

This was a fish I had never seen before—neither in the water, in picture books, nor in fish markets—yet I knew with utter certainty what it was. I had heard my father's friends talk in respectful tones about catching them on trips to Maine and Canada. This was a trout!

Admittedly, that six-incher was a Lilliputian sample, but it did qualify as "perfect." It was a member in good standing of a small, select group of closely related fishes that offer the angler every-thing he could wish for. This elite list is limited to the flowing-water, insect-eating trouts and, as we shall see, only a few species carry all the necessary credentials.

The Atlantic salmon (*Salmo salar*) and its landlocked form, which is no longer considered a subspecies, deserve the place at the very top of this honor roll. Both spend major parts of their lives in running water and are really just large trout, as their first name, *Salmo*, indicates. They are mainly insectivorous during their lives in rivers and, even though the sea-run form does not feed at all during its return to fresh water, its insect-eating reflexes are reactivated at this time and it is usually caught on artificial flies.

The major species of what are usually called the trouts qualify, too, even though they may chase a lot of minnows and crayfish during the gluttony of old age. The brown trout (*Salmo trutta*) is an excellent example, feeding mostly on insects during its first five or six years of life and often after that when the supply is abundant. So does the rainbow (*Salmo gairdneri*) and the cutthroat (*Salmo clarki*). Taxonomists keep declaring (and undeclaring) new species and subspecies from time to time, but there's not much point in making finer distinctions as a fisherman.

Of the trout-cousins called chars, perhaps only the speckled (brook) trout (*Salvelinus fontinalis*) should be included. The Dolly Varden (*Salvelinus malma*) of the West Coast is not principally an insect feeder, nor is the Arctic char (*Salvelinus alpinus*) of the North. The lake trout (*Salvelinus namaycush*) is unfortunately fond of deep water, and so are the several lesser-known chars of Europe.

Grayling, though they are even more distant relations of the true trouts, still deserve some consideration because they, too, sport the distinctive adipose fin of the tribe. They certainly prefer running water and they feed mainly on insects till they fall dead of old age. But, as we shall see, they fall short in other qualities and probably should be excluded. The Pacific salmons, six *Oncorhynchus* species, should be disqualified, too, since most are caught on heavy tackle in salt water and only a few are taken on insect imitations in fresh water.

From a scientific point of view, this grouping of fishes by habits makes little sense even though it does to the angler. Scientists might further point out that the selected fishes are not particularly smart, but merely shy, and that their place on the evolutionary ladder of fishes is down near the bottom rung, far below the relatively advanced catfishes. While I hold in great respect and awe any mental discipline that can put a man on the moon, I have to subtract a few points when it raises the catfish above the trout.

I am also aware that this selection may not exactly endear me to the army of trollers, surfers, bait-casters, or spin-fishers, either. In fact, I expect to hear accusations like "effete feather-fisherman," "trout chauvinist pig," or worse. And at this point, my chances of winning my case may seem as hopeless as Perry Mason's in the opening chapters. But stick around, there may be a surprise ending. I have a few expert witnesses and some devastating evidence.

First is the appraisal of history itself. Angling literature—which can boast of far more volumes than any other sport—has devoted more than half the pages in its library to this small group of fishes. For every book that has been written about bass, pike, stripers, or sailfish, there are two, three, or more on salmon and trout, and most of the famous books — and famous authors — throughout history have concentrated on these latter species.

Artists and illustrators seem to share this preoccupation with these same fishes. Trout and salmon are drawn and painted more often than any other species. They are, that is, if you can disregard the stylized carp that appears on so many oriental plates and vases (and I, for one, am perfectly willing to disqualify all crockery from the category of art).

A third field has also focused on this group of fishes. Fish culturists have devoted, by far, the greater part of their efforts, both in research and in actual propagation, to trout and salmon. Habitat-improvement attempts have also dealt almost exclusively with bettering their streams and rivers. Today probably eighty percent of all hatcheries—I mean true hatcheries, not commercial fish farms—raise these fish exclusively.

How has this select group of fishes managed to capture the imagination and inspire the efforts of the world of letters, art, and science for several centuries? And why have the trouts always been most prized by fishermen — at least in the countries where

226 / FLY-FISHING HERESIES

they occur in reasonable numbers? Simply because the list of virtues these fish possess is longer and more illustrious than the Boy Scout Oath.

The first quality that sets these fish apart is the manner in which they feed. To a very large extent, they subsist on insects and are readily caught on artificial imitations of these small, nutritious animals. Forgetting, for the moment, the joys and skills of fly-tying, this preference in food makes delicate, sporting tackle not only possible but nearly mandatory. You can't fish a small fly successfully on a heavy leader and you can't, in turn, keep from breaking a fine leader with a stiff, heavy rod. As a result, fly tackle is the most refined, most worried-over tackle in the world and because of its delicacy it is the least fatiguing to the angler and the most sporting in terms of magnifying the fish.

For example, I once killed a salmon of over twenty pounds on a small #10 wet fly. I had first rolled him on a sensible #6 and then gone to a #8, but under those low-water conditions he preferred to wait for the #10 before fastening firmly. Actually, I deserved to lose that fish because I choked and played him far too lightly and too long, but my point still stands. That's an awfully large fish to hook on a fly about a half-inch long.

Similarly, I once hooked a trout of between eight and ten pounds on a tiny #18 dry fly, and this was no fluke, either. I had seen him rising steadily to small naturals in the clear water and he wouldn't take till I gave him the correct color and size. In this case, however, I was robbed. I'm still convinced I deserved to land that fish, as I very nearly did, but that's a story in itself.

Nearly as important, it seems to me, is the fact that these fish live and feed in relatively shallow running water most of the time. The joy of small lures and light tackle would be canceled out if these fish hid themselves in the depths. The fight would bog down, and you certainly wouldn't dare use that three-ounce rod if your flies had to be lowered a hundred feet or more on metal line or with a sinker the size of a sash-weight. Then, too, you would miss the thrill of seeing the fish take as you usually do when fishing shallow runs and flats.

Another seldom-mentioned blessing of this type of fishing is that the game is usually played alone and on foot. The law may state that non-residents must hire a guide for salmon fishing in

Canada, but this is more a local employment scheme than a necessity. And, even though a few very large rivers are more easily fished from a boat for both salmon and trout, this is the exception rather than the rule. This ability to fish effectively without guide, crew, boat, outriggers, depth-finders and other intruding paraphernalia adds greatly to the joy and intimacy of fishing. There's a reward to this sort of one-on-one confrontation that is hard to describe, but veteran surf-casters will understand instinctively. Most of them would rather catch one good fish from the beach than a dozen from a boat. So would that small group of dedicated bonefishermen who prefer to stalk the flats on foot even though they know their chances would be better in a skiff with a good guide.

Certainly, any game fish deserving a top rating must have strength, style, and heart. The trouts rank very high in all three. Most species are acrobatic performers—salmon and rainbows especially. Yet browns and brooks, especially those in their early prime measuring twelve to eighteen inches, take to the air with surprising regularity when they're in peak condition. Admittedly, no trout will jump as high or as often as a tarpon. None will run as fast or as far as a bonefish. And none may give you the long, dogged, tugging fight of a jack. But even if trout don't win any particular event, they are all-round performers—probably the decathlon champions among fishes.

Trouts have one enormous energy source that is denied to almost every other freshwater fish: the ability to utilize the boundless pasturages of the oceans. Very few fish can migrate from fresh to salt water and back, but this is precisely what all the trouts, including the brook trout, can do. Running water has little or no plankton—a primary food-source at the bottom of the chain — and is, therefore, much less productive than still water. To make up for this, these fish will run out to sea, grow at a fantastic rate, and then obligingly deliver themselves back to your doorstep several times as large as they could ever get on river food.

Dams and pollution have cut off so many trout populations from the ocean that it's easy to forget this bonus, but all species will make this migration where and if this opportunity still exists. The mighty steelhead of the Pacific Northwest are only sea-going rainbows. The famous sea trout of Europe are merely sea-run

The Atlantic Salmon (*Salmo salar*), the fish that outshines all others, even its close and princely *Salmo* relatives.

browns. And the "salters" of Cape Cod and the "sea-trout" of Canada's Maritime Provinces are just brookies that have packed on the poundage during a season in the Atlantic.

This type of fishing rewards skill and punishes error because the quarry is shy and feeds selectively. This makes the capture of a trout especially rewarding. Yet if you choose the right fly and present it with delicacy and imagination after a cautious approach, you can succeed with pleasing regularity.

A complete novice might well hook into a near-record bluefish or striper on his first outing in a charter boat, but I'll lay you ten to one he couldn't catch a trout worth keeping his first day astream and he'd be lucky to catch a really decent one in his first full week.

Another amenity of trout fishing is that the fish tend to distribute themselves fairly evenly throughout a river, with every good lie holding at least a fish or two. When you approach a

The speckled trout (*Salvelinus fontinalis*), beautiful native of our eastern streams, from Georgia to the Arctic Circle.

productive-looking pool or run, you can be almost certain trout are there. It's up to you to figure out when, how, and on what they will be feeding. On the other hand, fish that school up make for feast-or-famine fishing—a lucky angler may make a killing by stumbling onto a wandering school while a more skillful one may go blank because the schools decided to avoid him that day.

Best of all, fishing for the trouts tends to become a way of life and leads the angler into more related hobbies and interests than any other sport. Certainly trout gear is talked about and tinkered with more than any other type of tackle, but that's just part of the game. I mean full-fledged hobbies in their own right. Fly-tying is a notable example. So is rod-building—especially for those few who still experiment with tapers and actions by planing their own raw bamboo. Entomology has been taken up by thousands of enthusiastic fly-tyers and flyfishermen. The truly dedicated even get involved in hydrology, geology, chemistry, botany, and the other disciplines that make up ecology in an attempt to understand more about their favorite waters, the life-systems they support, and how they can be protected or improved.

Even if you're not an angler, but merely a fish-watcher or fish-eater, you will still be drawn to the trouts. They live in the most beautiful waters of the world—cool, unspoiled streams and rivers. It's true that some mountain lakes are jewels, too, but these are usually trout lakes. Though an increasing number of our waters of all kinds have become soupy and shabby-looking, I have never seen a first-rate salmon or trout river that was not lovely to look at. For when man has butchered the trees the water is no longer cool. Where he has allowed dwellings to clutter and fester, the water is no longer pure. At this point salmon and trout quietly disappear as if they were part of an ethical boycott.

The outward beauty of the trout has been described so often that I need add little here. You may well think this praise has been overdone if you have seen these fish only in restaurant windows or in the baskets of friends who have followed the hatchery truck to your local creek. All these are hatchery fish, raised in sluggish tanks on artificial food, and they are cheap counterfeits, easily detectable on the line, in the hand, or on the table. Then, too, colors of all fishes fade soon after they die. To eyewitness these fish in their full splendor you must hold the wild ones in your hands at the moment of capture. Then, to steal a phrase from Izaak Walton, they are "Too pleasant to be looked upon, but only on holy-days."

The shape, or conformation, of the trouts is another joy to behold. We say a pickerel is skinny, a bass is deep, a carp is fat or a flounder is flat. But compared to what? Compared to a trout, of course. Unconsciously, we take the shape of the trouts as the yardstick against which all other fish are measured.

This may be hard to believe, but trout even smell good — at least they do when compared to most other fishes. Pike are notoriously slimy and bass have a skin odor that only a fisherman could love—which is why they are usually skinned before cooking. But I have never heard even a fastidious non-fisherman complain about the stench of a fresh-caught trout or salmon. A small point, perhaps, but add it to our total reckoning.

At the risk of being accused of overkill, I must add that the trouts are the most obliging of fishes even after their capture. They have no sharp spines or fins to puncture the unwary hand. Anyone who has been speared by the tines of a catfish—or even a small bluegill—will appreciate this. Trout lack the deadly dentistry of pike, bluefish or barracuda, too. And they don't conceal razor blades in their gill-covers as snook do, either.

Trout are pleasingly easy to clean. With pan-sized specimens, merely slit from the vent to the pectoral fins, free the tongue with an outside cut, stick your thumb into this newly created "mouth," and pull downwards. One good tug frees tongue, pectoral fins, and guts all of a piece. Now run your thumbnail firmly up the backbone to remove the jelly-like kidney and the job is done. No need to scale, skin, or fillet. You can clean four or five trout a minute without hustling in the least. Salmon are even easier to prepare, but we'll take that up later.

The flesh of the trouts is the most prized of all fishes with fins. Atlantic salmon is selling at over $3.50 a pound right now at my fish store—not much below Maine lobster. Trout would probably be equally dear except that wild fish may not be sold in this country and the white-fleshed, pond-reared fish sold to innocents by restaurants and fancy fish stores are as much like wild trout as supermarket chicken parts are like ruffed grouse.

Wild trout as well as salmon have orange or pink flesh when they are in good condition. The trouts store up future energy as a pinkish oil that is evenly distributed all through their flesh — a tidier, and certainly tastier, system than larding this surplus on the hips or bellies as do species we all know. This oil is what the salmon lives on during its several-month fast in fresh water; it carries the trout through the rigors of winters, and it makes dining on them both delicious. A spent salmon or a March trout will probably have white flesh—as does the synthetic hatchery model —and is fit only for chowder if you are unwise enough to kill it.

The Atlantic salmon—and the Atlantic salmon alone—goes even further to ingratiate himself to the angler. He delivers himself back from the ocean not only large, lively, and delicious, but with a built-in handle. His caudal, or tail, fin is so stiff when he is mature that you can grab the exhausted fish by the wrist of his tail, lifting him firmly and safely from the water at the moment of truth without the aid of a cumbersome net or disfiguring gaff.

And, as if that were not the peak of accommodation, he also has packaged himself as a hermetically sealed food container. To prepare a salmon for travel or storage, all you do is cut out the gills. There's no need to gut a salmon till you're ready to cook it and, in fact, it keeps better whole. Digestive juices stop flowing once a salmon enters fresh water, so the fish won't eat through its own belly while lying on the ice as other fish surely will. Then, too, bacteria which cause deterioration have a hard time entering the atrophied throat or penetrating the tough skin. I have kicked sawdust off summer salmon that have been lying in an ice-house for six weeks or more and found them every bit as firm and good as the day they were landed. Try keeping any other fish a mere six days, ungutted, and you'll appreciate this trait of the salmon all the more.

And that pretty much winds up my case for the trouts. History is witness to the fact these fishes have dominated sporting literature, art, and husbandry. The qualities that have raised them to this preeminence are the following: They take small food and lures . . . they live in shallow, intimate waters . . . they can be caught alone and on foot . . . they are superb fighters . . . they grow large at sea and then return to their freshwater home . . . they reward the skillful and escape the bungler . . . they spread out over the river in predictable lies, thus reducing the element of pure chance . . . their pursuit leads into other fascinating hobbies and studies . . . they take the angler to the most scenic waters . . . they are beautiful themselves in both color and shape . . . they are safe to handle, relatively pleasant to smell, easy to clean, and delicious to eat.

That's a staggering list of virtues, isn't it? I can't think of another fish, or group of related fishes, that rates half as well in even half these categories.

But don't these fish have at least one fatal flaw? Isn't there some skeleton in the *Salmo* family closet that I am hiding from you? Yes, I'm sorry to say, there is. Salmon are too scarce and most trout are too small—a condition that has been with us for many decades.

Nearly a hundred years ago, the Reverend Myron W. Reed was lamenting, "This is the last generation of trout-fishers. The children will not be able to find any." He was very nearly right, but his timetable was a bit off. He couldn't know that the durable and elusive European brown trout was about to be introduced into our depleted Eastern waters or that the American angler would soon have automobiles and aircraft to carry him to the untapped fisheries of our own West, Canada, and Alaska. The good minister was probably spoiled, anyway. Most of us today would drool at the quality of fishing he was saying the last rites over.

But the facts remain: Our present-day trout are often pitifully small. The average fish taken is probably under ten inches long, but this is the fault of over-fishing, not of the fish. Just look at the sizes these fishes can attain when given a decent chance. The record brook trout is 11½ pounds—almost exactly the same size as the record smallmouth bass. The record rainbow (51 pounds), cutthroat (41 pounds), and brown trout (39½ pounds) are nearly twice the size of the biggest largemouth ever landed. And the heaviest rod-caught Atlantic salmon (74 pounds) tops the biggest muskellunge, the species usually considered the largest of all freshwater gamefish.

I can't think of anything more to say in behalf of the trouts, unless it's this paraphrase of the famous saying by the Elizabethan physician, William Butler: "Doubtless God could have made a better fish. But doubtless God never did."

# Index